Chris Casson Madden's
new american
living rooms

Chris Casson Madden with Carolyn Schultz

Chris Casson Madden's
new american
living rooms

CLARKSON POTTER/PUBLISHERS
NEW YORK

Much love and special thanks to the men in my life—Kevin, for his support and advice; Patrick, for understanding; and Nick, for helping out on so many shoots.

As always, I owe much to Annetta Hanna, my editor, for her ever-astute advice and diplomatic deadline reminders.

I am indebted to my photographer, Nancy Hill. I'm in awe of her great vision and talent. Carolyn Schultz organized and executed so much of this book. Thank you for being with me every step of the way. Many thanks to Agnes Rethy, Pam and Kirsten Jordan, Marie White, and my wonderful office staff.

Douglas Turshen designed this book and, as always, hit just the right notes. And, of course, thanks to Nora Negron. Thanks to the great team at Clarkson Potter, especially Lauren Shakely and Barbara Marks.

Many thanks to Lynn, Richard, India, Giselle, Robin, Sally, Kathleen, Kathy, Mari, and Marcia for going beyond the call of duty and helping take care of our crew.

Thanks to James and Jennifer D'Auria for luxury accommodations.

Carolyn wishes to thank Mia, Claire, Brandon, and Lily for taking care of one another when she was away, and Andy for his loving support. Thanks to Ruth and Mel Miller for being there when needed, and to Eleanor and Glenn Dodds for loving and caring for the children when the parents weren't at home.

Nancy wishes to thank William and Montgomery and all the people who lent support to her, including Florence Hill, Charles Glaser, Venetta Williams, Ann Megyas, Bob Sweet, and Paula Yount. Thanks to Rick for his encouragement, humor, and weather reports. Thanks to Richard for the gold cards, and to Ernesto, Salvador, and Antonio for conjuring the best light. Thanks to Nick and Alice at Lens & Repro, and Ray and Walter at Photo Habitat. Thanks to Mark and Cathy at CT Photographics for their Super E.6, to Sally, Tom, Debbie, and Larry, and all those people who held gold cards, including Robin and Jeffrey.

Published by Clarkson Potter/Publishers, New York, New York.
Member of the Crown Publishing Group, a division of Random House, Inc.
www.randomhouse.com

CLARKSON N. POTTER is a trademark and POTTER and colophon are registered trademarks of Random House, Inc.

Printed in China

Design by Douglas Turshen

Library of Congress Cataloging-in-Publication Data
is available upon request.

ISBN 0-609-61002-3

10 9 8 7 6 5 4 3 2 1   First Edition

introduction

WHEN I WROTE *A Room of Her Own: Women's Personal Spaces,* I didn't realize at the time that I was embarking on such an incredible journey. That book, and the resulting speeches and book tours around the country, afforded me the pleasure of speaking to and, more important, listening to women describe and discuss how they, too, had set aside, or yearned to set aside, a space for personal pursuits. The idea had been planted—women need to create for themselves a sanctuary and a place for renewal in their homes. That discovery led to still more discussions with people about their quest to create spaces where not just women but couples, families, and friends could gather together to refresh and renew their spirits. My next book, *Getaways: Carefree Retreats for All Seasons,* explored houses, rooms, fishing shacks, garden structures, and tree houses—wherever it was that a group of people could come together and experience a sense of being "away." Then began an exploration of that most intimate of rooms—the bedroom. In *Bedrooms: Creating the Stylish, Comfortable Room of Your Dreams,* I gave readers not just a cursory glimpse into the bedroom, I tried to provide the grand tour—opening closets and drawers and pulling back the covers.

In my latest expedition—*New American Living Rooms*—I was privileged to take a close look at the way Americans live at home today in their most public area. The adventure of finding and documenting these rooms took me and my team around the country—from New Mexico to North Carolina, California to Connecticut, Georgia to the rugged mountains of Vermont and the coast of Maine. I wanted to be exhaustive in searching out these living rooms, to discover not just what they have in common but how homeowners have designed them for their own individual needs.

There are common threads in the contemporary American living room. This room is about community, about multitasking and pursuing many activities in a single, large space—a modern concept, yet one that embraces many historical references. We are hearkening back to a time when families regularly ate together and took their entertainment together, when the common room encompassed a place to dine—whether it was for breakfast, tea, or a casual or formal dinner—while at the same time housing books and photographs, musical instruments, or a table for cards and games.

The new American living room now sets the tone for the rest of the house. Often the room is grand in scale, with high ceilings punctuated by exposed or painted beams, slanting ceilings, skylights, or clerestories. Often there is a fireplace that matches the generosity of the rest of the room. Kitchens ease their way into many of these spaces, either with an island and counter seating, with appliances designed to blend in easily with the rest of the decor, or simply through the presence of a wet bar and refrigerator. Multiple seating areas, built-in bookcases, and entertainment units that disguise our electronic options are also part of the plan. Chaise longues, chair-and-a-half seating for two, oversized ottomans, banquette window seats, and kick-back daybeds are some of the furniture choices that are finding their place in a space that once featured only a sofa, a coffee table, and a pair of club chairs. The new American living room is, most importantly, about light, space, and comfort. It is about the way we live now, affirming that home is where we want to be, the destination we long for, and the place we belong.

contents

LIVING LARGE

barn
refound

SOME PEOPLE LOVE old barns and outbuildings the way others are fascinated by old trains, roadside diners, or autos. Beyond the aesthetic appeal lies the urge to lay claim—to rebuild and restore these artifacts of the American past. Often-times, it is not to their original purpose that restoration plans beckon. Rather, it is to showcase them so that others might

share the appreciation and respect felt by their owners.

"We found this early-nineteenth-century barn in New Hampshire that was going to be torn down. I knew I had to have it and that I would find a place for it somewhere," says the homeowner who now lives elegantly in that barn. "It was disassembled and placed in storage

and remained there for several years. It was only after we bought our current home that I knew what I was going to do with the barn."

After attempts to reconcile her decidedly traditional country style with the modern Japanese-influenced home she had recently purchased in a community thirty-five minutes north of New York City, the homeowner decided to tear down a portion of the new acquisition and reconstruct the barn in its midsection.

Drive by the newly renovated home and the barn might not be immediately apparent. The barn's siding was replaced in the front of the house by an indigenous stone façade, rendered in the Federalist style. But step through the front door and the magnificent framework of the barn is dramatically apparent in a room forty-five feet long with ceilings thirty-one feet high, warmed by large stone fireplaces at either end. The siding at the back of the living room has been replaced by huge expanses of mullioned, floor-to-ceiling windows and a pair of doors that open onto a rear courtyard, a scenic wooded lot, and the requisite babbling brook.

The outsized great room draws the family to congregate in the communal center of the house, leaving to its perimeter the kitchen, bedrooms, and baths. A huge chandelier is proportional to the space and reinforces the Federalist style of the exterior. The entry table serves as a divider for the different areas of the room. On one side is an enormous dining table set in front of the hearth with a collection of early American and English chairs, eighteen in all, gathered around. A smaller nineteenth-century card table set for four offers a more intimate dining spot next to the door to the kitchen.

PRECEDING PAGES: Blue-and-white porcelain complements the summer fabrics and slipcovers. A mix of woods and furniture styles adds distinction to each grouping. Area rugs also vary in color, size, and origin. LEFT: Drapery fabric adds softness and dimension to the large expanse of mullioned windows. An antique wing chair is covered in nineteenth-century fabric. Two trunks serve as a side table, while an upholstered bench doubles as seating and table space.

On the other side of the entrance is a seating area that relates to another fireplace and a television cleverly tucked into the bookshelf. A cozy conversation grouping is arranged in front of more bookshelves, suggesting this might be a quiet reading spot as well.

A more formal, salon-type seating arrangement is placed behind the entrance table, in front of the large windows overlooking the garden. In this area, fluid drapery stands in for architectural detailing, arranged over the rough-hewn support columns of the barn.

The sofas, armchairs, benches, and antique pieces in the seating areas create a separate look for each grouping, but white denim slipcovers accented by vintage blue-and-white ticking fabric tie them all together. Multiple area rugs—antique Orientals and well-worn kilims—also connect the various groupings in the room while giving those areas definition. The rich colors of the rugs are the perfect layering over eighteenth-century floorboards rescued from a winnowing room in Pennsylvania. Extensive collections of books, art, English blue-and-white ironstone, tortoise-shell boxes, tea caddies, and found objects warm the space with personality.

There is much to love about a barn—its humble origins, history, hand-hewn character, rustic simplicity, and grand scale. Reconfiguring it in a newer home gave this homeowner the satisfaction of preserving the best of America's architectural past and blending that heritage with modern life.

ABOVE: A detail of the paneling of old book spines at one end of the room, which conceals a television/ entertainment unit. RIGHT: Two tables offer dining options. A large table seats twelve to sixteen guests, while more intimate dining, for four or six guests, is available at the gateleg tavern table. An oil painting hangs in front of a display of books in the library wall. The doors to the kitchen are concealed behind the book spine paneling.

There is much to love about a barn—

OPPOSITE: A flat-screen television completely recedes behind a wall of books when not in use. Mantel sconces are electrified hurricane lanterns. CENTER, TOP: A red leather tabletop holds tortoiseshell boxes, a mahogany tea caddy, and a tole lamp. CENTER, BOTTOM: An antique child's chair complements a settee in this reading corner. ABOVE: An old garden urn is kept with a seasonal array of flowers, welcoming the visitor just inside the front door.

its history, simplicity, and grand scale.

bel air
beauty

THE KAPLAN HOME in Bel Air, a posh neighborhood in the
hills of Los Angeles, was designed by one of the city's premier
architects, Paul Williams. Williams sat on the first Los Angeles
planning commission in 1920; built homes for movie stars,
moguls, and financiers; renovated and reworked the Beverly
Hills Hotel with its trademark pink-and-green exterior; and
contributed to the futuristic Theme
Building at Los Angeles International
Airport (LAX). He designed and built
churches, banks, offices, and civic cen-

ters throughout the United States and the world, but he was best
known for the stunning simplicity of his residential designs and his
mastery of elegant traditionalism. He was also African-American,

the first black man elected to the distinguished American Institute of Architects (AIA) College of Fellows.

Honoring the home's historic pedigree, L.A. designer Lynn von Kersting has crafted a living room that remains true to its original aesthetic but yet is fresh, open, and eclectic—infused with European, Middle Eastern, and Old Hollywood decorating influences. Recalls owner Tracy Kaplan, "What is so wonderful about the house is the location, the views, and the property. We overlook the Bel Air Country Club and have incredible views of the Westwoods and lower Bel Air. At night we sit in our living room and watch the lights sparkle over the landscape and the planes coming into and out of LAX. It is a great vista of sky and air. However, when I met Lynn and saw her work, I realized what was missing here was her style. She gave us her signature look with the living room."

The living room opens grandly just beyond the two-story entrance hall and dominates the first floor of the Kaplan house. "Our children think of it as our 'talking room,'" says Kaplan. "We have children in bedroom wings on either side of the living room and we can hear if a child is up at night. They are all within earshot, so my husband and I relax in here in the evenings, knowing the children are fine."

Walls upholstered in a cheery red toile punctuate honey-hued floors, painted woodwork, and painted panels. Shaped like a T, the wide, central part of the room is divided into two seating areas. One is in front of a fireplace with the other in a sunny nook surrounded by a bay of windows. The furniture in these seating areas is an eclectic mix of sofas, slipper and arm chairs upholstered in nineteenth-century French fabrics combined with Moorish and Indian side tables, Chinese trunks, and pillows, floor cushions, and lamp shades covered in eighteenth- and nineteenth-century fabric.

At the top of the T, a door leads into a bedroom wing of the house. An ivory baby grand stands ready for the youngest members of the household, children not yet five, to start taking piano lessons. On the other side of the doorway is a fabric-draped table laden with family photographs, mementos, and treasured souvenirs, including a nineteenth-century French model of the Eiffel Tower. It resides

PRECEDING PAGES: A collection of nineteenth-century Moorish tables are inlaid with mother-of-pearl. Colorful garden roses fill an antique tole bowl. A nineteenth-century slipper chair is covered in antique Indian fabrics, while nineteenth-century pillows are plentiful on all the furniture. OPPOSITE: The designer removed the top doors from this armoire and lined the back with a mirror to display rare, first-edition books, shells, lacquer boxes, and nineteenth-century French botanicals.

Honoring the home's historic pedigree, the

design remains true to its original aesthetic.

next to what appears to be a closet behind a paneled enclosure until the panel is raised and a wet bar is revealed.

"The wet bar is one of our favorite features of the room. It is original to the house and came fully equipped with granite counters, copper sink, and hanging cupboards for glassware. The house was built during Prohibition so the bar had to be concealed. The panels are motorized. with one push of a button you can open or close the panels, depending on which guests you've invited that night. We use it now as a place to serve drinks before our Friday dinners when our parents, nieces, and nephews come over for Family Night," explains Kaplan.

At the other end of the room, tall bookcases flank the door leading into the entrance hall. On one side, French doors next to the bookcase open onto an outdoor seating area and the fragrant rose gardens beyond.

"We had the bookcases already in place," says Kaplan. "They were sitting there, nearly empty, with a few knickknacks. Lynn took off the top doors, painted them, and, in her inimitable style, brought them back to life."

Tracy could not be more pleased with the collaboration that took place, albeit decades apart, between architect and designer.

"I love being in this living room," says Kaplan. "It takes me back to my childhood when I would visit my family in England. The size and grandeur of the room is brought into human scale with the multiple seating areas and the layering and richness of the fabrics, prints, paintings, furniture, and personal treasures. Just sitting in here becomes an experience."

PRECEDING PAGES: The scale of the room allows for two generous seating areas. The Prohibition-era bar in the upper left can be concealed behind sliding panel doors.
OPPOSITE: A baby grand piano is topped with an opaline vase filled with garden roses, a nineteenth-century Venetian music stand, blue-and-white porcelain, and a red tole tray bearing a candelabra dripping with crystal.
RIGHT: Lemonade is served from the Prohibition-era bar.

adirondack
pleasures

AT THE TURN of the twentieth century, privileged families were retreating to great camps in the Adirondack Park region of upstate New York, a wilderness of rugged mountains and picturesque lakes. High society flourished in the area until about mid-century, when many of the well-heeled found that "The Park" had lost some of its glamour and appeal.

At the turn of the twenty-first century, new families are drawn to the Adirondack region for its lack of glamour and pretension. They seek to maintain the traditional aspects of Adirondack living, appreciating the area's regional vernacular, the comfortable society of casual get-togethers, and the four-season recreational pursuits.

Local artisans did much of the detail work,

PRECEDING PAGES: A grand three-
tiered antler chandelier and a
fieldstone hearth are the two great
focal points in this room. A mix
of French, American, and Moroccan
fabric motifs combine in a bold red,
white, and blue statement. OPPOSITE:
A granite counter separates the
kitchen from the rest of the room.
A work station with computer, fax, and
phone is concealed in this cupboard.
ABOVE, LEFT: Detail of a cupboard
door. ABOVE: The television occupies
its own built-in niche.

including wood carving and crafting furniture.

Scott and Molly Ford are a young couple seeking to establish a great camp of their own in Lake Placid, New York, for their children and the generations to come. They hired local architect Michael Bird and his firm, Adirondack Design Associates, to create a home that is a modern rendition of the classic camp. Bird designed for them a cluster of large, rustic buildings including a boathouse on Lake Placid, a main house, a guest house, and a barn. These are all rendered in the style of the region: the structures, with multiple pitched-peak roofs, use indigenous wood, stone, and decorative touches of peeled bark, twigs, and branches.

Bird has a particularly strong sense of history, having grown up in the Adirondacks. He is interested in not only preserving the local architecture but also improving upon its design, imbuing it with openness and light.

In the early camp homes, rooms tended to be dark because they were wainscoted in natural wood or logs, and heat loss made large windows impractical. Bird, however, carefully plans the placement of windows. In the Ford guest house, the design includes large, thermal-paned windows and a clerestory of diamond-shaped windows beneath the roof gables. A skylight built into the steep pitch of the roof also floods the room with light.

LEFT: Skylights in the pitched roof at either end of the great room and strategically placed clerestory windows offer a profusion of light to what might otherwise have been a timber-darkened room. Planed pine on the ceiling is also effective at reflecting light back into the room. On the wide-planked floors, area rugs separate seating areas. Concrete architectural finials have been fashioned into lamps on either side of the sofa.

Mari Kirwood Bird, Michael's wife and an interior designer, helped the Fords with the interiors throughout their camp. She employed local artisans to do much of the detail work, including the carved panels on the built-in cupboards, and much of the twig furniture, including the chest behind the sofa and the tables beneath the windows. Bold, graphic red-and-white and blue-and-white fabric combinations refer back to classic American motifs.

In the open plan of this house, the kitchen, dining area, and seating in front of the hearth all seem to radiate from a central point anchored by the large antler chandelier in the middle of the room.

"What Michael and I do is to interpret the comfortable, relaxed lifestyle of the Adirondacks for our clients," says Mari. "The woods, mountains, and lakes that surround us are the real inspiration."

carriage
house
revisited

WHAT HAPPENS when the expectation is to be to the "manor" born, but the carriage house seems so much more appealing? You simply move in. "Originally the carriage house was to be a guest house," explains William Hodgins, the venerable Boston designer, of his client's Southampton abode. "However, as plans and decorating progressed, it seemed that the carriage house was more interesting and appropriate, and wonderfully convenient for the owner's lifestyle."

The large, two-storied carriage house is set in an idyllic expanse of trees, greenery, and manicured lawn with the Hamptons signature tall hedges in front and a long, pea-gravel lane leading to the front door. The carriage house was originally built around 1910, one of several service buildings for the large shingle-style cottage next door.

What the clients found more fitting for their weekends in the country was the relaxed openness the carriage house provides. Time spent with family and friends takes place in one convivial, communal space—big enough for large gatherings and lively, comfortable conversation, but with cozy, intimate spots in the corners of the room for one-on-one discussions and private reflection.

The original doors still slide on antique hardware tracks to open and close the room from the front entrance. In the middle of the space that once housed horses and buggies is a generously sized library table. With its freshly picked bouquet from the gardens, the ample round table is always a noteworthy spot for the latest books and periodicals. Upholstered skirted benches anchor the table at the four compass points.

"Signature touches in this family room are the large, classically styled bookcases—freestanding furniture rather than built-ins," explains Hodgins. "This room didn't need to be constrained by built-ins. Rather, there is flexibility and mobility in this arrangement that allows for the reinterpretation of the space when there are large social gatherings or special events."

The room demands big pieces of furniture, and Hodgins obliged with another signature touch: oversized chaises, ottomans, tables, and chairs all in neutral, harmonious creams, whites, and beige, anchored by carefree sisal carpeting.

The room has the look and feel of a garden room despite the

PRECEDING PAGES: The original carriage house doors make a grand architectural statement as they open the room to the front entry and the garden beyond. A large central library table holds fresh bouquets and plentiful stacks of books and magazines. Upholstered benches surround the table and are easy to pull into any of the other furniture groupings. RIGHT: An architectural medallion crowns the mantel. Large, neutral-toned furniture is one of the designer's trademarks.

The room is connected to an idyllic expanse

of trees, greenery, and manicured lawn.

large, upholstered furniture, the classic details on the bookcases and over the mantel, the abundance of books, and the lush drape of fabric over the table and in the throws. Perhaps it's because of the huge pottery urns filled with flowering plants that stand sentry beside the sliding glass doors. Or maybe it's the column fragments that serve as end tables or the expanses of glass unadorned except for slender matchstick shades. In any case, this room combines the best of both garden and interior salon. It is a library with an out-of-doors feel, a dining room that is not quite al fresco, and a casual room that has overtones of formality.

"It is the perfect place for weekends in the country, to share with a widespread circle of friends who stay—comfortably and happily—for weekends and weeks at a time," notes Hodgins.

PRECEDING PAGES: Simple matchstick shades and a classic architectural ornament over the free-standing bookcase are signature Hodgins touches. OPPOSITE: A nineteenth-century painted sideboard is the perfect scale to the other oversized pieces in the room, including the dining table with a pedestal center. LEFT: A nineteenth-century French jar stands on the poured concrete mantel. ABOVE: A custom-designed bookcase that rises almost to the ceiling is flanked on one side by an oversized concrete garden urn filled with flower pots and on the other by a simple picket-slat side table.

mountain
greenery

THE DREAM HOUSE for a family of avid skiers would certainly be on a mountain, steps away from the top of the slope. After a day spent careening down its summit, the family is welcomed home with the enveloping warmth of a wood-paneled room, a bright fire, and a soft sofa.

Architect Mark Finlay and interior designer Julia Durney teamed together to realize this dream home in a Vermont ski resort for their clients, a family with three children and lots of visiting family and friends.

Built on Stratton Mountain in Vermont, the home was designed with a nod to the local Vermont vernacular. It resembles the older homes indigenous to the area and capitalizes on the natural materials that complement the grandeur of the mountain landscape—a snowy white in the winter, a verdant green in the summer.

The home's slate paved entry hall opens up to an expansive, fir-paneled living room, the main gathering spot for the family après-ski, as well as for holiday festivities and summer reunions. An open floor plan permits views to the kitchen and dining area on one side of the living room and to the stairs leading up to the library loft and the master bedroom suite on the other.

"The house is casual to fit in with the homeowners' lifestyle," explains Durney. "They definitely wanted a fun house and one that was easy to care for. Those two criteria dictated a lot of the choices."

Bluestone, slate, wood paneling, exposed beams, and simple tiles are all natural materials that don't require much maintenance. The Adirondack-style furniture is lighthearted and impervious to the occasional snow-soaked bottom or wet boot.

Much of the furniture, including the dining table and chairs, armchairs, console, and coffee tables, were custom made in North Carolina of unstripped hickory wood. Several pieces were also embellished with twig designs and carvings that add uniqueness as well as a touch of age.

The furniture was deliberately arranged for multi-generation use. The living room comprises two seating areas, one facing the large fieldstone hearth and the other facing a custom-built, fir-paneled entertainment armoire that houses a TV and electronic games. Upstairs overlooking the great room is a small library niche. Complete with its own warming hearth and plenty of books and games, the area offers solitude and peace, a quiet place to slip away yet still feel connected to the gathering below.

Durney, Finlay, and the homeowners worked closely together to create this vacation house. "Because we conceived of it jointly it has a seamless quality. There is a consistency here that comes from having ordered all the lighting from one source, all the hardware from another, and all the furniture from one locale. Using resources like that helps you develop a plan and a design that remains true to its mission. It doesn't become clichéd or cutesy," explains Durney.

PRECEDING PAGES: Back-to-back leather sofas offer the choice of hearth or entertainment viewing. Steps at the back of the room lead to a cozy reading area complete with its own hearth. BELOW: Adirondack appointments. BOTTOM: A leather chair awaits a reader. OPPOSITE: A view from on high shows the relationship of the kitchen and dining area to the sitting areas. A wall of windows welcomes plenty of light and great mountain meadow views.

down-east
essence

SALLY AND TOM SAVAGE both grew up in Maine and their

roots there have held them fast. That is not to say that they

haven't experienced other parts of America or the world. They

also have a residence in Florida, and they lived for a time in

Europe so Sally could study languages, painting, and finishes. It

is just that the Savages are adept at pursuing their passions and

Maine happens to be one of them.

The Savages built their dream

house in an old whaling seaport on the

foundation of Tom's grandparents'

1911 home overlooking the protected waters of Boothbay Harbor.

Tom inherited the property but found the house had not borne

well the effects of time and the harsh Atlantic coastal weather.

"The old house was poorly winterized and damaged by mold," explains Sally. "We built this new house where the old one stood. It keeps the spirit of the old house but I was drawn to European interiors. So I blended the two. This house is a combination of Maine cottage and European farmhouse."

Their home is also a story about recycling and reclaiming the past. A sympathetic restorer took the old home apart and sold it for salvage, but not before Sally and Tom had a ceremony "to thank it for being what it was, a family home and a good friend," says Sally. The restorer was also instrumental in helping Sally and Tom find the missing pieces for their newly built home.

"We were looking for beams and we met a craftsman who took down old houses and sold the architectural pieces," says Sally. "He had even developed his own tools for dismantling and reassembling. Through him we found the old barn that we used for the beams, as well as the china closet doors and old French doors for the porch.

Wherever possible we incorporated architectural salvage to give the house an older feel."

This borrowing from the past is evident throughout the house and particularly in the open floor plan of the living room, kitchen, and breakfast area. In this large space antique terra-cotta tiles reclaimed from roofs and floors in France echo the patina of the old barn beams in the soaring ceiling. The imposing mantel, constructed of hand-carved coquina stone from

PRECEDING PAGES: The light-filled, spacious room combines the elegance of a European manor with the informality of a country farmhouse. Barn beams on the ceiling and ancient tiles underfoot provide rusticity, while a coquina hearth, Pierre Frey fabrics, and an oversized entertainment armoire provide luxury. OPPOSITE: A breakfast nook has stunning views of the Maine coast. LEFT: Sally's own hand-painted plates and bowls perfectly complement the setting.

Mexico, looks aged by virtue of its material and its high-quality craftsmanship.

Another element that suggests a centuries-old European farmhouse is the generous use of hand-painted dishes, lamps, frescoes, and framed canvases. Sally was the creative force behind most of these items.

"I developed a fascination for old French, Italian, and Portuguese pottery. These artisan items inspired me to re-create their patterns and motifs on my own plates and tiles," Sally explains.

Sally has created a business with her artistry. In the winter months she teaches classes in fabric finishes, decoupage, mixed media, and pottery glazing in Ocean Reef, Florida. Her work has found its home in Maine, however. Here the shelves and cupboards are stacked with her pottery designs, plates, mugs, and bowls while oversized platters are hung on the walls and displayed on armoires and hutches.

The Savages have also brought touches of Florida with them to Maine. The house design was borrowed from a home they visited in Florida. Sally modified the design by adding large rooms on either side of the house so that both she and Tom would have personal spaces, his a study to pursue business interests, hers a studio to paint, draw, and design.

As for the furnishings, "the antiques were all found locally here in Maine," says Sally, "but the newer stuff and reproductions have mostly come from the Design Center in Miami."

The painted panel portrait over the mantel looks like a European antique but it was actually painted by a Florida artist on a wooden medallion. The custom-sized armoire was adapted for their large-screen television, and the coffee table was also custom designed and enlarged to add balance to the armoire.

It was once said that fine art lies in the melding together of hand, head, and heart. By this measure, Sally and Tom Savage have mastered the fine art of living in a home in which the hand, head, and heart truly are united. Sally has imbued their home with her own art and design and her own brand of eclecticism. And about their passion for this northeastern shore: "Maine is a place of the heart for us," says Sally. "We both grew up here and it is where we have family. This is the place we come home to."

OPPOSITE: A pass-through to the kitchen offers a preview of hand-painted pottery and other country kitchen elements. An armoire contains more of Sally's artistry and her collection of European crockery. The pillar was faux-painted to resemble Italian marble. Sally painted the pear using egg tempera. Guy Chaddock designed the rush-seat bar stools for the Oliver Walker Showroom in Florida.

SERENE LIVING

santa fe
soliloquy

TO FIRST-TIME VISITORS to Santa Fe, the constant sunlight reflecting off red dust and adobe walls may seem a bit oppressive, especially if the heat and dust are accompanied by traffic noise, road construction, and the confusion of one-way streets. But be patient, for the charms of Santa Fe are hidden, lying in wait to surprise and delight the visitor who is lucky enough to step behind those old resi-

dential walls.

At James Blackwell's abode in Santa Fe, the distance from the driveway just off the street to the gate leading to his front garden is a mere fifteen feet, but it may seem as if you have been transported to another time and place. Once inside his enclave the light and

dust of the desert are gone. The garden seems to offer perpetual shade and calm. Step into the house embellished with art and antiques, and the quiet is awesome, reminiscent of the hush of a chapel, offering respite for the soul.

A historic home in a town with, by American standards, a long history, the slant-roof adobe house was originally built more than 120 years ago. Elizabeth "Betty" Stewart, an architect of the last century who took on the construction of adobe and claimed it as her medium, bought, expanded, and renovated the structure, preserving the pitched room that makes the dwelling unique in a town of flat-top adobes. She also gained renown as a local character, known for her outspoken opinions and eccentric lifestyle. The house she built and lived in suited Blackwell just fine.

"When I first walked in this house, it was magic," he says. "The living room was empty except for the sconces. I told Susan DuPépé, my decorator, that the place had the feel of a monastery. Susan said, 'Let's hang our hats on that proposition and use lots of religious art,' which I just happen to love. I think it's because I'm the end of the line in my family and when you don't have kinfolk you gotta have angels."

The religious art is tempered with just the right amount of the secular and the profane to make the living room liveable. In some instances, a tableau or vignette, such as the Day of the Dead sugar beads draped over a religious reliquary, demonstrates a touch of black humor as well. "Both Susan and I have southern backgrounds," laughs Blackwell, "she's Cajun and I'm from Texas. You can't escape humor with that combination."

The room may suggest a chapel in a mission compound complete with a stiff-backed bench flanking one wall, but otherwise the furniture avoids any associations of church pew discomfort or cold, stiff knees; it is deep, oversized, and inviting.

"It was Susan who suggested we divide the room into particular areas," says Blackwell. "We established an area for the music room, bounded by the carpet, and I knew I wanted a place for people to just chit-chat."

DuPépé convinced Blackwell not to place a pair of conventional sofas in front of the hearth. Instead, a love seat faces a pair of massive leather chaises longues on either side of the fireplace surround. A large, low table in front of the love seat is adorned with books and reliquaries.

PRECEDING PAGES: A pair of elk antlers found in Colorado are placed dramatically over the mantel, drawing the eye toward the ceiling and emphasizing the pitched roof, unusual in this historic district. The monastic feel of the space is emphasized by the many reliquaries and other religious art. OPPOSITE: Blackwell's collections of Bolivian and Mexican silver crowns and chalices, family pictures in silver frames, and ceremonial fabric are displayed on the vintage baby grand piano.

Unsure of how the layout was going to work in a social gathering, Blackwell invited friends for cocktails and a musical evening before committing to the arrangement. "I told everyone to just make themselves at home," he says. "And you know, they all ended up on the chaises and sprawled on the couch. That's when I knew the room really worked."

Music plays a central role in Blackwell's life. Cajun, Cuban, and classical music emanate from a CD player stored in the eighteenth-century console. The grand Steinway piano, laden with crowns, *santos*, and family photos framed in Mexican silver, is a cherished family heirloom: once belonging to Aunt Rosa, it was presented to young James in 1958.

"When I was in the tenth grade I was given the choice. I could either have a Thunderbird or the piano. I took the piano. I wanted to be a concert pianist. But when I got it I realized I had the inclination but not the talent," confesses Blackwell.

His musical ambition was not for naught. On the board of the Santa Fe Opera, Blackwell hosts fund-raisers and gala musical events at his home, with local and visiting artists providing the talent and Blackwell the appreciative ear and hosting skills.

Like many good southerners, James Blackwell is a storyteller, making conversation another important part of his evenings with friends and acquaintances. Though the living room contains stunning paintings and other works of art, Blackwell notes, "People sit and talk, or listen to the music. They don't pay attention to the art. They're just here having a good time. In fact, when people do compliment me on my living room they say two things, that it is perfectly in balance and it is restful. They feel at home."

For a man with angels for kinfolk, that feels just about perfect.

RIGHT: An oversized leather chaise is juxtaposed with an eighteenth-century Mexican bench in the conversational area of the living room. French doors lead to an exterior courtyard where a fireplace keeps the chill at bay. A pair of applewood twig chaises were crafted by an artist in Taos, New Mexico.

urban
serenity

THE VIEW from the thirty-fourth-floor window of Marie and David Ritter's New York City apartment would thrill even the most jaded denizen of the Big Apple. In one panoramic vista you can see west across the Hudson River to the New Jersey Palisades and east to the waves of the Atlantic as they hit the shores of the Far Rockaways. Step out onto the terrace and New York City can be viewed from an eagle's perspective. From here you could call in a traffic report for the streets and bridges, check the punctu-  ality of the Metro-North trains running in and out of the city, or look down upon the rooftop playgrounds of countless elementary-school children. You can see it all but what you feel is simply peace.

"We found that when we traveled, the places we liked, the places we were drawn to were always minimal or spiritual," recalls Marie, reflecting on the design of her city home. "When there is so much going on outside in the urban environment, so much stimulus and activity, then I feel it is important to have a serene space to retreat to, where you can go home and process everything that happens. For me, this is that place, a space almost spiritual in its serenity."

The Ritters have lived in their building for several decades, but the present incarnation of their space is just a few years old. It was a revelation to them that they could actualize their dream house, the one that they envisioned through the editing process of life, travel, and experience, in the same space where they had raised three children in what Marie describes as "your standard, three-bedroom cookie-cutter apartment."

"When our youngest started college we started thinking about the transformation of this space," says Marie. "I think the kids were surprised that we took over their bedrooms. But ultimately, it was a nice lesson for them to see what was possible."

The architect and designer who helped the Ritters see the possibilities was Bruce Bierman. "I actually saw a picture of his own loft in a magazine," says Marie. "I thought right away that this is someone who respects small spaces. After a year interviewing architects and designers we met with Bruce and knew that he was the one to help us realize our dream."

Bierman began by gutting the apartment and raising the living room atop a platform that at once added dimensionality, a step up into the room, and much more of a horizontal perspective, which was instrumental in creating the serene, harmonious space. Low furniture, including a monochromatic greige sofa, love seat, and chaise on one side of the room, provides a quiet space for reading and reflection. A pale celadon sofa faces an entertainment unit on the other side of the room with additional space for a desk, computer, telephone, and other electronic equipment.

Between the two halves of the room, multiple shoji screen panels were cleverly designed to be used as a room divider or, when pushed back, to add a note of architectural interest. "One thing that surprised us," recalls Marie, "was the way the light is softened and warmed as it passes through the shoji. We find that we tend to close the screens more in winter, to divide the space in two. I suppose it is the hibernating instinct, to enclose the room with warm light, or perhaps it's our version of a hearth . . . it makes the room feel really cozy. In the summer we open them for brighter light and air."

The shoji screens are practical as well. "They really do keep the sound out. When the TV is on, they mute the noise and I can sit on the other side and read and not be disturbed," says Marie.

However, the secret to this room's minimal elegance lies not in the furniture, the well-chosen accessories and plants, or the transparency of the shoji screens. It is hidden behind every seeming wall or panel. The secret is storage, strategically placed everywhere, painstakingly planned to meet every need so that all the necessities of living—the office paper clutter, the books, the complex sound and entertainment systems, even the refrigerator and coffee maker—are stored and hidden from sight. This is Bierman's real genius and his signature design style.

"We had our plans on the drawing board for over a year so that every little detail was accounted for," says Marie. "I did give away a lot of stuff accumulated from living here for twenty years. Still, I kept things that mean something to me and it is all here, within arm's reach."

For the Ritters, this is living as good as it gets. As Marie says, "Walking through that front door makes me happy. Here there is order—everything in its place, peacefulness and serenity. We want to always live in the urban environment. We enjoy being a part of it. It is just nice to have a buffer, a place to come home to."

OPPOSITE: The quiet side of the shoji-divided room features this conversation area and a chaise from John Saladino in front of the terrace window. ABOVE: No window treatments obscure the view from the thirty-fourth floor looking toward the East River. Leather desk accessories from Arte Cuoio, Italy, complement Holly Hunt's Polo desk in walnut.

vermont
hideaway

SEVERAL YEARS AGO my husband, Kevin, and I realized a

decades-long dream when we purchased a weekend home in

the idyllic village of Dorset, Vermont. The house is a little gem

that was built in the 1960s by an enthusiastic modernist. With

its soaring floor-to-ceiling living room windows and sharply

angled rooflines, it might seem more comfortable in Palm

Springs than in our apple orchard nes-

tled between the Taconic Range and

the Green Mountains of Vermont.

Although we loved the more for-

mal feel of our circa-1911 home in the New York suburbs—with

its traditional arrangement of living room, dining room, library,

and kitchen—we both felt a twinge of excitement at the thought

From breakfast to late in the evening, this

PRECEDING PAGES: A slipper chair, pedestal table, and wing chair from the Chris Madden Collection for Bassett Furniture combine effortlessly with the clean lines of a Federal Sheraton sofa covered in Jack Lenor Larsen fabric. OPPOSITE: A Vermont slate counter separates the kitchen from the dining area. ABOVE: Chris's sister, Marybeth, painted the portrait of Chris and Kevin in the sixties.

is a soothing, convivial gathering room.

of combining in one enormous (at least to us!) space living, dining, kitchen, and entertaining. I soon realized what a treat it was to be able to prepare drinks and dinner in our kitchen while across the room our sons played a heated game of Scrabble and our guests read and relaxed in front of the brick fireplace. A country farm table can accommodate up to sixteen, making it the perfect spot for large gatherings.

As is the case with most homes in the mountains, the focal point of the room is the fireplace, and our favorite spot is the generously proportioned sofa that I designed for my Bassett Furniture collection. A large glass coffee table, usually cluttered with books and magazines and bowls of popcorn, is flanked by two easy chairs covered in a soft cream chenille with African-motif pillows.

A large "gaming" table (actually a round dining table) is adjacent to a classic Sheraton sofa I acquired many years ago. The sofa accommodates extra Monopoly players or on a quiet afternoon affords the perfect spot to read and enjoy the mountain views.

LEFT: Slipper chairs in the dining area surround the manor table from the Chris Madden Collection for Bassett. Natural slate flooring throughout unifies the kitchen, dining, and seating areas. Sisal carpeting helps define the seating area in front of the large brick hearth. The Dorset sofa from the Bassett collection is covered in a paisley fabric that offers a burst of color in the otherwise neutral space. Hydrangeas were clipped from the surrounding gardens.

I designed one of my favorite pieces with inspiration from an antique walnut "Beau Brummel" that we have at home. Originally a shaving sink for English dandies at the end of the nineteenth century, it has been refashioned as a stylish bar, complete with a built-in ice bucket in the "vintage" metal sink and a wine rack beneath.

Designed primarily for pleasure, our new living room is also an informal gallery of photography and artwork by family and friends. My younger sister's oil painting of Kevin and me adds a light-hearted touch over the mantel. Some black-and-white photographs that I took of Rye Playland in Rye, New York, during a record-breaking blizzard hang over the "Beau Brummel," and my younger brother Jim's extraordinary color prints are on an adjacent wall. More creations by friends add a personal stamp to this setting.

From breakfast at the kitchen bar to late in the evening when the last embers of the fire are flickering, this is a soothing gathering room for our family and friends.

desert
sanctuary

THE PHRASE *cathedral ceilings*—a Realtor's description to inspire visions of a room grand in scale and ambition—doesn't necessarily conjure glorious images of Notre-Dame. In fact, in many homes, cathedral ceilings are a liability, with windows too tall to dress and walls too massive to induce intimacy.

A remedy to those misplaced ceilings can be found at the

home of Jim and Rebecca Long and their three children in Albuquerque, New Mexico. Here is the apotheosis of a cathedral ceiling, a room in which

the other elements enhance the grandeur of the architecture, and the ceiling style becomes an apt description for the sense of awe that is invited by this living room.

"Finding this house is what kept us in Albuquerque," says Jim, a successful entrepreneur with businesses in Albuquerque, Santa Fe, and points in between. "We had been house hunting in Santa Fe and really thought we'd settle there until we came upon this house called 'La Concha,' the shell."

For the Longs, finding the house was indeed like finding a magnificent shell whose definition had been lost over the years. Built in the mid-1980s, it had grace, beauty, and a wonderful structure but it was lacking in detail. Fortunately, time spent house hunting in Santa Fe had introduced the Longs to the interior design work of Susan DuPépé. "We kept seeing these wonderful homes decorated by Susan," says Jim. "Her style and philosophy matched what we had in mind for our own house."

The Longs, both of whom were born, raised, and educated in New Mexico, were very clear in defining and articulating their vision of the home they wanted to live in. Proud of their heritage and the Spanish and Native American influences in their state, the Longs sought to evoke Spanish Colonial style but modify it to meet the casual life of a busy family. They felt this could best be accomplished by pairing the antiques, art, and contemporary furnishings of many different cultures with locally made artisanal crafts, finishes, and techniques. Their house would then offer strong visual interest with comfortable and inviting living spaces. They succeeded on all counts most admirably.

The first thing that commands attention as you step through the grand entrance doors is a stunning altar piece above the mantel

PRECEDING PAGES: The grand scale of the architecture is modeled after eighteenth-century Mexican haciendas. The altar by master carver Victor Goler over the mantel commands attention and respect.
LEFT: The massive coffee table is of Cantera stone from Mexico. Naturally formed in a range of hues from rose to lilac to brown, the stone is used throughout the house, from the mantel and support pillars in the living room to the flooring throughout.

created by Victor Goler, a master carver in Taos, New Mexico. In the undertaking the Longs had purchased "Our Lady of Guadalupe," one of the *bultos* (a three-dimensional *santo*) ensconced in the altar. Over time, the Longs acquired other *bultos*, and before they began work on their house, they commissioned the artist to build an altar for their collection.

"What is wonderful about the altar is seeing how the artist's style evolved over time. Goler carved it in stages, one *santo* at a time," explains Jim. "It took him years to finish it. When the altar was brought into the living room it was received with the same respect that is accorded an altar installed in a church or chapel."

"We actually had a ceremony where the priest came and 'enthroned' the Sacred Heart of Jesus," says Rebecca. "This is a tradition when an altar is put in place. The priest places the sculpture of the Sacred Heart in the middle of the altar. We had our family and friends attend and then we celebrated with a fiesta in the backyard."

The living room itself is a large square located in the center of the house several steps down from the hallway that frames it and the rooms that surround it. This arrangement turns the living room into a sort of interior courtyard, surrounded by a protected loggia. To gain access to the other rooms in the house you are given the choice of stepping down and through the living room or proceeding around it.

The room is divided into five areas suited for different activities. There is the main seating area in front of the altar and the hearth consisting of two sofas, a pair of chairs, and a very large coffee table of cantera stone from Mexico. A grand piano, purchased from an opera singer who retired in the area, defines another space, as does a game table in one corner, a small conversation area in another, and a children's corner complete with books and an antique school desk from Mexico.

Throughout, the living room contains furniture from Europe, Peru, Mexico, and New Mexico. Behind the sofa stands a seventeenth-century Peruvian refectory table with *bultos* carved by Eduardo Sanchez of New Mexico. In the small conversation

BELOW: Four carved wood chairs surround a nineteenth-century Spanish game table with an embossed leather top. OPPOSITE: A painting of the Virgin Mary is flanked by iron sconces in a niche that conceals a tiled wet bar with an ice machine, sink, and glass storage. An eighteenth-century bench from Mexico is fitted to hold wine jars.

area, a seventeenth-century Spanish arms chest serves as a coffee table. The gaming table is Spanish with chairs of hand-tooled embossed leather seats and backs and nailhead trim.

And then there is that ceiling. Local craftsmen arranged small pine poles or *latillas* to cross the ceiling like a rustic mosaic, imbuing the room with a sense of age. Vaulted clerestory windows were cut into the adobe walls beneath the ceiling to add light and dimension to the soaring space. Beams and corbels were left exposed while cantera stone columns add support and bring the focus back down to earth.

Jim personally coordinated the talented team who worked on his house. DuPépé assisted in the interior design, choosing the colors, fabrics, and materials; Richard Martinez was instrumental in the building design; and T. Alan France ferreted out many of the antiques and other furnishings from Europe and Central and South America. John DeMars and McKenzie Croft, faux painters, did the glazing on the walls, giving them the luster of an ancient building.

Jim and Rebecca Long have expressed in their home their abiding appreciation for the heritage of New Mexico. They have created a place that is both rich in history and full of life. They are not living in a museum; rather, they are living in a constantly evolving tribute to those who have come before them.

OPPOSITE, LEFT: Tintypes are a favorite
collectible. OPPOSITE, RIGHT: A detail
of the altar and the *latillas* that cross the
ceiling. ABOVE: A Spanish arms chest
with nailhead trim, circa 1650, stands
between a pair of antique bishop's chairs
from Argentina in this quiet seating
area. The mesquite bench is from Mexico.
New cathedral-size candlesticks were
finished with an antiquing glaze. The
painting of the Ascension of the Virgin
is nineteenth century.

metropolitan
aerie

WHEN YOU LIVE in a high-rise building in a crowded city full of similar structures you might well feel isolated from the world of nature. But when one wall of your living space is glass, with multiple sliding doors opening onto a terrace dozens of floors above the ground, you can have a very lively sense of the world outdoors. While not the nature of verdant gardens and leafy trees, nature in a high-rise apartment becomes the sky, and light becomes your indicator for more than just the time of day; it also  signifies the weather and the seasons. Clouds and sky evoke an ever-changing landscape of colors, sounds, and scents.

Homeowner and entrepreneur Jack Karpus has carved out his

own space in the sky, an apartment aerie for weeknights in the city and special weekends with his family. Atlanta decorator Bill Cook helped him achieve a modern, spare look with a design that complements the dramatic view beyond the terrace.

The focal point of the spacious, four-bedroom condominium is the open floor plan that encompasses an entrance hall, entertainment and conversation seating area, dining table and buffet, and pass-through to the kitchen. Blessed with Atlanta's temperate climate, the outdoor terrace expands the living area immeasurably.

"The whole high-rise environment lends itself to clean lines and a more minimal approach to decorating," explains Cook. "Having worked with Jack before, I knew he appreciated sleek and modern design especially because it complements his extensive collection of modern art and black-and-white photography."

The living room holds a small sampling of Karpus's collection of art, photography, and sculpture. One of the most important pieces in the room rests on a pedestal near the dining table, a sculpture by William Morris, a protégé of the famous glassmaker Dale Chihuly. "I like to look at shapes and how they interplay and work together," says Cook. "Jack's pottery is mostly a collection of monochromatic whites that reveal the simplicity of their forms."

PRECEDING PAGES: A blown-glass sculpture by the artist William Morris rests on a corner pedestal near the dining area. Jack Lenor Larsen striped fabric was mitered into squares to cover the pillows. OPPOSITE: A B&B Italia coffee table reflects a collection of art pottery and glows with the luminous light spilling from a wall of glass in this high-rise overlooking the skyline of Buckhead. A pair of chairs are by Richter. The shag rug is from Myer's Carpet.

With their curvaceous lines, the pottery and the Morris sculpture offer relief to the otherwise angular room. The furniture is laid out in a grid, with the sofa, chairs, tables, and entertainment unit embracing the rectangular or the square and mirroring the grids in the wall of glass.

"When we were coming up with the design and arrangement of the furniture Jack and I decided to forgo custom furnishings in favor of simple, clean-lined modern pieces. These can be moved easily around the room when Jack entertains or when his family is visiting," says Cook. "Jack also didn't want extraneous furniture to detract from his art collection."

Light and shadow are the predominant design elements in this peaceful, monochromatic space, with the colors of the sky providing the perfect backdrop.

"The high-rise environment lends itself to

OPPOSITE: The painting by John Reilly is titled *Ménage à Trois.* The entertainment wall unit is by Met Design, and the black-and-white photographs are part of an extensive collection. ABOVE, LEFT: An interesting play of texture, shape, light, and shadow surround these monochromatic forms. ABOVE, RIGHT: A kitchen is connected to the living room by a pass-through with bar stools from Hothouse Design.

a more minimal approach to decorating."

LIVING IS EASY

faded
fancy

DONNA KAPLAN'S HOUSE is in the glamorous Bel Air section of Los Angeles, but its ambience is more suggestive of other locales, the South of France, perhaps, or the Caribbean, depending on which room you're in. The house is nestled into a hill, sited beside a brook that rushes alongside the windows of the living room, creating the constant backdrop of a pleasant-pitched gurgle. Little walk-ing bridges punctuate the stream as it winds down the hill. The living room has worn surfaces and an eclectic mix  of furniture, objects, and nineteenth-century fabrics that seems to place it in another time and country.

"It is my favorite room in the house," says Kaplan. "Even though the house itself has a French farmhouse feel, this room makes me think of the Caribbean—a place we visit quite often. The colors remind me of the ocean and the relaxed Caribbean lifestyle. Here we can hear the brook and the insects in the garden since the French doors open onto the patio and pool deck."

Kaplan bought the house, originally built in the 1930s, in the late nineties. "It was a 4,900-square-foot home, French-style with a mansard roof," recalls Kaplan. "When I walked onto the property, I hadn't really thought of creating a French farmhouse, but I looked at that series of bridges crossing the stream and I couldn't help but see the resemblance to Giverny. I did a lot of research into the French country look, gutted the house, and had it almost entirely rebuilt to my taste and specifications."

The result is an elegant, relaxed rendition of French vernacular architecture with eclectic interiors that transcend any particular region or country. Decorator Lynn von Kersting, who is also the owner of Kaplan's favorite shopping haunt, Indigo Seas in Los Angeles, helped Kaplan achieve the soft, cheerful look in her living room.

"Lynn's real strength is in her ability to mix things up. She has a set decorator's knack for arranging a room and letting the objects speak volumes about who you are and where your tastes lie," says Kaplan. "I am an avid collector and I have a good eye, but Lynn can come in and put things together like nobody else. Her signature is mixing the precious with the not-so-precious. Ultimately, it is the furnishings, the accessories, not the architecture, that make

PRECEDING PAGES: A seaside cottage is invoked by the shell-encrusted mirror and lamp. LEFT: The zinc-topped bar is a French antique. RIGHT: Nineteenth-century chintz fabrics cover a pair of club chairs in this cheerful room. A Victorian wicker coffee table stands between a pair of linen ticking-striped sofas. The roses in the antique French jar are from the surrounding gardens. A profusion of pillows from Indigo Seas are all made from eighteenth- and nineteenth-century fabrics.

the room. The appointments are what people respond to and fall in love with."

In the corner stands a tin-topped nineteenth-century bar from a storefront in Provence. Two red-striped sofas provide comfortable seating for settling in with a drink. The wall unit at the back of the room houses a big-screen television amid nineteenth-century majolica, old advertising signs, and nineteenth-century French market baskets.

Together Kaplan and von Kersting have made the room sing. As Kaplan notes, "This room speaks to me because it is not so ornate that it takes away from the furnishings, antiques, and collectibles that I love so much. And for me, it is the small things that make the house truly a home."

OPPOSITE: The display of a fine collection of eighteenth- and nineteenth-century majolica is enhanced by interspersing the shelves with antique oil paintings on canvas and board and with old French advertising signs. BELOW: The relaxed room does not try to disguise its generous number of electronic gadgets, including a big-screen TV and DVD, video, and CD players. CDs and DVDs are contained in French market baskets lined with nineteenth-century linen towels stacked on the lower shelves.

endless
summer

WITH ITS ROLLING DUNES, ramshackle paths, and miles of sandy beaches, Fire Island has provided generations of New York City families a welcome respite from summer in the city. The island is a hodgepodge of distinctive communities and equally distinctive architecture.

On one of Fire Island's more remote stretches, designer

William Hodgins—of the renowned Boston firm of the same name— worked with a New York City couple to create a weekend getaway for them and their family and friends. Built in 2000, the house sits on a plot of beach at the very tip of the island, in a quiet neighborhood of other beach homes.

"The family wanted a cottage that fit the beach community and looked as though it had been there awhile. This was accomplished by building in the local vernacular—shingle-siding, large wrap-around porches, and mullioned windows," says Hodgins.

With large windows on three sides and doors opening to the terrace, the living room captures every ray of natural light and seems to hug the outdoors, catching the breezes and salt spray.

The furniture is an eclectic mix of natural materials and textures—wicker, rattan, bamboo, painted pine, and oak placed on a sisal carpet. The furnishings all seem indigenous to the place, as if they were grown there, plucked from the sand, and placed inside. The colors of the sofa, chairs, and cushions match the colors of the outdoors: soft tans, blues, shades of white and green.

The walls are adorned mostly with mullioned windows. Where there is a solid wall, you are likely to find built-in furniture for storage or amenities. Against one of these, a wet bar offers refreshments with a well-stocked refrigerator of sodas and mixers and a separate ice maker to fill the glasses before taking them out to the terrace. In another, banquette seating fronted by an antique refectory table provides a cozy spot for gazing at the view, enjoying a meal, or catching up on some correspondence. On a wall opposite the entrance is a painted buffet that holds more pleasures for

PRECEDING PAGES: A white-painted piano offers the promise of late-night sing-alongs. A terrace surrounds the living room on two sides, with a front entrance door on one side and double French doors on the other. LEFT: The living room includes all the amenities of summer living—a banquette dining area, a cozy conversation area, and a portable, cushioned game table. A nineteenth-century nautical painting of a storm at sea adds visual weight to the room.

children and adults: books, games, decks of cards, and art supplies.

Square cushions stand at the ready to be used as a table for an impromptu game of Chinese checkers or as floor cushions inside or out, for those who prefer to lounge.

"This is a getaway house for a family with young children and lots of friends and family on their guest list. The house is open from the deck to the kitchen, with space for all kinds of activities and pursuits," says Hodgins. "It is a house for casual living, that lets your imagination open up—and it requires little maintenance and preparation."

The living room captures every ray of light

OPPOSITE: A wet bar with refrigerator offers convenience and style.

ABOVE, LEFT: A Chinese checkers board stands ready for action on a stack of square-cut cushions.

ABOVE: A rattan chair and ottoman, floor lamp, and side table create the perfect reading spot. An antique globe signals a contemplative mood.

while it catches the breezes and salt spray.

key west meets east

JOE BLOUNT KNOWS a thing or two about having fun, in style, and his living room in the Hamptons proves it. Take the painted palms on the walls and the decorative palm fronds spilling out from the painting above the mantel. "My good friend and decorator, John Oetgen, decided I needed something distinctive on these walls, a little bit of Key West, so he just got up on the ladder one morning and painted them," says Blount. "Free hand. Had it done in several hours. He just thought it would be a fun touch."

Or take the custom-made thirteen-foot-long sofa studded with pillows and the equally massive low coffee table that fronts it. "The sofa will easily accommodate two overnight guests if they decide not to leave after a party," says Joe. "Or it can seat a half dozen or more guests who can put their feet up on the coffee table."

That is, if they are not engaged in a rousing game of Gin or Liverpool at the card table, or seriously listening to some of the eclectic tunes that emanate from the stereo speakers hidden behind their faux painted disguises, the pots of the frescoed palms.

Joe Blount, along with Chip Cheatham, is owner of Pierce-Martin, a national design company based in Atlanta, Georgia, offering wicker, rattan, hand-forged iron goods, lighting, and other home decorating items found in their travels in the Pacific Rim—the Philippines, Indonesia, Thailand, and Hong Kong. In their company as in Blount's home, newly crafted production pieces are combined with ethnic, one-of-a-kind antiques and other treasures from around the world.

Joe Blount met his decorating pal John Oetgen in Atlanta. They are both southerners inclined to see the humorous side of a situation, and both admire each other's work. Even though the living room was a recent add-on to the house by the former owners, it was still subjected to the Oetgen touch. The soaring ceiling height and tall windows looking out to the pool and garden gave the room an ethereal feel but not a lot of architectural weight.

"John remedied that by fattening the beams on the ceiling," says Blount. "We also added the chandelier and the pediment over the fireplace to give some visual cap to the tall space."

While the sofa and coffee table were custom-made for the room, most of the furniture is from the PierceMartin collection. True to his design philosophy, Blount has some unusual touches

PRECEDING PAGES: The room is taller than it is wide, with floor-to-ceiling windows and a balcony overhang creating a cozy niche for built-in bookcases and a table for reading or games. RIGHT: A thirteen-foot-long sofa almost dwarfs the teak and rattan Indonesian coffee table in front of it. All the furniture is from PierceMartin. Equally large books under the table are antique French ledgers, containing census information for a county's worth of cattle and sheep.

ABOVE: The table is a hollow-based antique zinc restaurant table from France. Awnings and pull curtains provide shelter in the outdoor extension of the living room. The candle chandelier is operated with a pulley for easy lighting. OPPOSITE: The flooring in the outdoor living room is preformed concrete, cut into individual tile blocks and then laid with grout.

that give the room personality and punch, including a Thai rain drum used as an end table, a pair of English house ornaments on the mantel, and antique mirrored sconces that break into the painted trunks of the palms, reflecting light and adding sparkle when the candles are lit for an evening gathering.

The library shelves hold art and reference books and novels. "This is where I come to read," says Blount. "In the morning I bring the paper in here; otherwise it's lovely to build a fire and spend the afternoon with a book."

French doors make a graceful transition from the palm-painted living room to the outdoor poolside space. Here, the seating area is defined and protected by a canvas awning shell and curtains that can be pulled to fully enclose the room or tied back, adding an elegant drape to the corner posts. Storage areas were built to house the essentials of outdoor living and entertaining: undercounter refrigerator and towel storage in one, a wet bar, complete with sink, ice maker, and shelves lined with elegantly styled acrylic glassware in the other.

Like his indoor living room furniture, the furniture outside is also from Blount's PierceMartin collection. One-of-a-kind exceptions include an antique, galvanized round French bistro table and a pair of architecturally carved stone lamps from Indonesia.

In the summer the patio doors are left open, making the out-of-doors another easily accessible room in the house. "I work from out here, making calls into the office and reading reports. But being out here makes it not like working," says Blount. "It is like vacationing at home every day."

hollywood
al fresco

IN AN IDYLLIC CLIMATE like that of southern California, when your home is protected by the hills of Hollywood and tucked within a lush garden compound, you can afford to do something most of us only dream of: live in a house turned virtually inside out. In the typical house, a hard outer shell of mortar and brick, wood, or stucco offers a protective exoskele-

ton surrounding the soft spaces and accoutrements of living. In Lynne Wasserman's home, plush and expan- sive outdoor seating, dining, and entertainment areas encircle the actual structure of the house so that the exterior walls become display areas—a place to hang majolica plates, nineteenth-century tole trays, and shell-encrusted

PRECEDING PAGES: Portieres can
be drawn to give a sense of enclosure
to the space. An eclectic mix of
fabrics and textiles is a von Kersting
trademark. ABOVE: An étagère
displaying pottery and plants makes
use of an exterior wall as a display
area. OPPOSITE, LEFT: A dragon-
motif needlepoint pillow made by
Wasserman. OPPOSITE, RIGHT:
Sun-warmed tomatoes and French
sea salt are a perfect outdoor
appetizer.

mirrors and shelves. Windows and sliding glass doors provide access and views into the interior rooms.

Lynne Wasserman, daughter of the late Lew Wasserman, the legendary Hollywood talent agent, president of MCA, and philanthropist, is a child of Hollywood who grew up among such notables as Alfred Hitchcock, George Cukor, and Billy Wilder. A mother of two children, now grown, Lynne has taken up her father's philanthropic fund-raising and political activities.

She enlisted the help of designer Lynn von Kersting, whom she met socially about ten years ago, to help pull together her modern California-ranch-style home. Von Kersting used vintage red and white fabrics, pillows, and nineteenth-century French and Moroccan furniture and dishes, from her Los Angeles store, Indigo Seas, to create an outdoor space that is casually inviting, yet visually exciting. A large American flag pulls all the colors together and imbues the outdoor living room with nostalgia. Lush ferns and draping vines, dense bougainvillea, ripe fruit, fragrant flowers, and garden-warm tomatoes all lend themselves to the allegory of endless summer.

Upholstered furniture, plump cushions, fine fabrics, area rugs, books, candles, chandeliers, glassware, and china—the same treasures one would expect to find indoors are out here, barely contained under the cantilevered roof, spilling out into the gardens and into the pool area beyond.

"I do everything out here," says Wasserman of her loggia living room. "I love being outdoors— reading, dining, gardening, swimming, and entertaining. My outdoor living room works perfectly."

southwest
soleil

WITH GOLDEN SUNLIGHT streaming in from skylights and playing off the fresh blue and white fabrics, the summertime appeal of Charlie and Barbara Young's Santa Fe home is apparent. "It is sort of Santa Fe meets Provence," says Barbara. "Our home reflects our love of travel and the places we visit." Besides frequent visits to France, the Youngs have also traveled extensively in Mexico. "You either love it or you hate it and we happen to love it," Charlie notes.

Born close to the Mexican border in Arizona, Barbara has always had an appreciation of the culture and art in Mexico. Her mother, an accomplished painter who contributed the painting of sunflowers over the Youngs' mantel, didn't start painting until she was forty-two. "I was thinking at the time that she was kind of old to start a new hobby," laughs Barbara. "Now, of course, that seems young."

The Youngs are aptly named; their story is really about how it is never too late to do anything. They fell in love late, having already been married with two children apiece. And they recently decided that after Barbara survived two bouts of cancer it was never too late to buy a second home and create a getaway to enjoy with their combined family and friends.

Several years ago they found their home, built by J. C. Nichols in the 1980s, in the heart of Santa Fe, close enough to walk to the Plaza. With the help of their contractor and master builder, Sonny Otero, of Taos, New Mexico, the Youngs added built-in cupboards by the fireplace to house the television, and shelves and cupboards in the game-table area to display collectibles and for storage. The built-in furniture has traditional detailing with iron-work hardware and willow twig inserts on the door panels.

Through mutual friends, the Youngs met interior designer Pam Duncan from Wiseman & Gale & Duncan Interiors, who helped iron out some difficulties they were having in the arrangement of the room. "I wasn't used to having big, open rooms that look into one another," explains Barbara. "Pam helped us realize that the high ceilings can really throw off your dimensions."

Duncan helped the Youngs create a new

PRECEDING PAGES: A Turkish rug softens the terra-cotta floor. The coffee table was made by Abydos in Taos. RIGHT: A flower bowl reflects soft summer color. OPPOSITE: A games table that is a reproduction of an antique mah-jongg table sits in front of a hutch and shelves crafted by Sonny Otero of Taos, New Mexico. The willow inserts, called *sombraje,* are a decorative touch. Shelves hold a collection of *milagros,* collectible pottery, and large blue-and-white jars from Mexico.

ABOVE: An English picnic hamper serves as an occasional table between two slip-covered club chairs. The stacking tables beside the sofa were an inheritance from Barbara's mother's travels in the Orient. OPPOSITE, LEFT: Gingham-checked ottomans tucked under a console table provide extra seating, table space, or leg comfort. OPPOSITE, RIGHT: *Milagros,* or little miracles, are symbolized by the brass charms and figures on the crosses. The one with blue stone is from San Miguel de Allende in Mexico.

living room arrangement that works, encompassing a seating area for conversation and media entertainment, a game table juxtaposed with library shelves, and a sliding door to the exterior courtyard. Duncan also helped them choose fabrics to coordinate with their inherited collection of nineteenth-century blue-and-white Japanese Meiji platters and their collection of Mexican jars. Blue and white accents complement the white cotton duck slipcovers on sofa and armchairs. A custom-built coffee table, by Abydos in Taos, adds the refined rustic touch that this eclectic room demands.

While everything about this room suggests summer and sunlight, cool breezes and lavender scents, one of the best memories the Youngs have of being in this room was when their family gathered and they put up their first Christmas tree.

"We had just moved in. We didn't have any ornaments yet for the tree. We went to town and bought angels with canvas bodies and tin wings and decorated the tree in bright New Mexican colors. Santa Fe was quiet, there was a fresh snowfall, and we decided that this is how Christmas should be. This was where we wanted to gather as a family."

DESIGNED FOR LIVING

the reading
room

THE FOUR WALLS in this rectangular room seem to soar in a space that is taller than it is wide. One wall is a bank of windows that makes the gardens outside seem touchable and the two dogs romping in the yard appear almost to be in the room. The fireplace wall, a massive, white canvas anchored at the bottom by a solemn, recessed hearth, is simply framed  while a third wall is a montage of art and sculpture. The fourth wall most resembles a grand altar in a modest-sized cathedral. Here, the object of worship is books—art, architecture, photography, history, and the novel are celebrated in an architectural stack that rises to the ceiling, flanked on either side and at the top by slender strips of glass.

This is the living room of John Lineweaver and John Oetgen, an Atlanta designer whose signature is exuberance and whose style is as fresh and tangy as a piece of ripe citrus.

"This room is a stage set for the things I've collected over the years," says Oetgen. "I love the verticality of the space—all the light. It's the great white box that I was looking for, the one I've wanted— it is kind of a laboratory, a room in which to play with our things.

Oetgen and his partner recently moved into the house with their two bearded collies, Cody, the elder, and Flizo, the puppy, after spending the last several months with a team of workers painting walls, redoing floors, redesigning a kitchen, and building bookshelves.

Originally, they were set to build their own house, of Oetgen's design, but they ran into a real-estate glitch. Rather than facing more delays, they went out looking for a house they could buy. Craving space, light, and tall ceilings, Oetgen knew that a more modern structure would probably best suit him. He was pleased to find it in his current house, built in the late 1970s by the Atlanta firm London/Taylor, known for their spare designs in a city that favored more southern elegance.

PRECEDING PAGES: The designer relaxing in his living room. LEFT: An unusually long, semicircular Louis XIV canapé anchors the library end of the living room. The tall sculpture was created by Oetgen for an AIDS benefit in Atlanta. Two custom-made slipper chairs provide seating for dining at a nineteenth-century Florentine marble tabletop set on an antique column base. A sculpture by James Hull, based on the groin vault of a cathedral in Florence, is on a pedestal behind the dining spot.

"I was discouraged about finding a modern house in Atlanta because there just aren't that many. However, when I saw this house I knew it would work. We made some structural changes and did a lot of renovation, but I felt immediately that this house captured the essence of my design aesthetic."

What excites Oetgen about the house are its minimalist qualities, the dimensions of the rooms, and the light.

Because the living room furniture is not set up symmetrically or based on any grid or squares, it seems to flow through the space, defining different areas in a fluid, casual manner. The most striking piece in the room is a semicircular sofa, a French Louis XIV canapé that Oetgen found on one of his shopping trips to Europe.

"It was so huge, I flipped," says Oetgen. "I bought it in Paris and I've left it just as I found it, with the brown cotton velvet upholstery highlighted by the pale turquoise edging. It downplays the elegance of the piece with just the right note." A pillow, covered in a silkscreen of a Roy Lichtenstein print, adds a jolt of vibrancy and modernity to the canapé.

Floating near the center of the room, creating a visual, almost architectural break, is a sculpture made by Oetgen, once used as a totem for AID Atlanta, a charitable event staged by leading Atlanta designers. Nestled in front of the fireplace wall are a pair of Oetgen-designed chaises, a Francois Lalanne table in the shape of a bird, entitled "Berry," and a pair of eighteenth-century Swedish arm-chairs. Four French surgical lamps on casters provide lighting in the room where and when it is needed.

Clustered on a wall above and surrounding a circa-1940s chest by the French designers Jules and Andres Leleu is a sampling of Oetgen and Lineweaver's extensive collection of art.

"I think collections should be gathered together but arranged in mayhem," explains Oetgen. "They can take over one area, as I did with this wall."

Oetgen enthusiastically mixes periods and styles when he mounts a grouping of art. Sharing equal billing on his wall are pieces by Picasso, Degas, Warhol, Sonia Delaunay, and Todd Murphy, and a Lichtenstein framed paper plate.

This is a room that is at once playful and serene—a light-filled space in which to read, entertain, or simply relax.

BELOW: Capturing some of the voluminous light and throwing it back, splayed, onto the hanging art pieces are four Plexiglas, multicolored rectangles by Vasa standing atop the dresser. RIGHT: The dining spot faces the garden. A sculpture of an eighteenth-century satyr stands upon his pedestal.

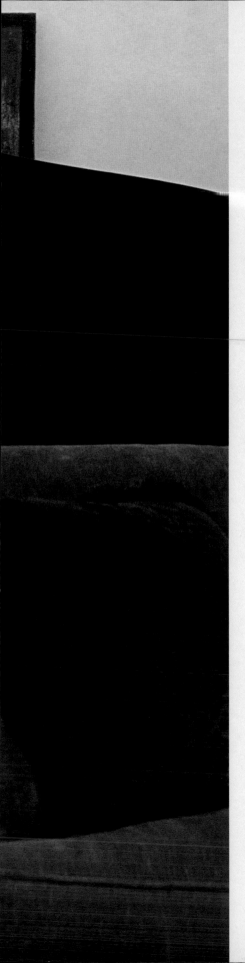

retreat

ENTERTAINMENT LAWYER Julia Sorkin and her husband, Aaron, the writer and executive producer of television's *The West Wing,* have carved out a comfortable home for themselves and their young daughter, Roxy, in the Laurel Canyon area of Los Angeles. Working with Martin Lawrence, owner of the design firm Martynus, Julia Sorkin shopped the flea markets and design centers of Paris, London, New York, and Los Angeles to create this handsome sanctuary.

"I found Martin after interviewing about ten people," says Julia. "When I saw his design portfolio I knew he was the one for me. A few weeks into the project he was going to Europe to visit family and I was going to Paris to attend a wedding so we decided to meet up for a shopping expedition. We found some wonderful things and came away with lots of good ideas."

Asked to describe the look that she and Lawrence devised for the house, Julia laughs, "It's romantic. It's evocative. But I love the way Martin describes it best: 'The look says it's Italian, but darling, I love to travel.' So I guess we have a basic Italian country look with an antique French fireplace surround and a nineteenth-century English dining table put into the mix. I think it's perfect for California.

"The house was completely modern when we moved in," continues Julia, " with a slate fireplace and a wood-paneled entry. It was very spare. We put in the moldings and baseboards, faux-painted the walls, and darkened the floors. We added the romance that we felt was lacking."

The Sorkin house is situated on a hill. The land in front of the house is terraced straight up the hill while in the back a lushly planted garden has steps leading down to an outdoor living room, pool house, and writing studio. To accommodate the slope, the entrance hall steps down into the living room and more steps lead into the dining area. That, in turn, opens to the kitchen on one end and a covered patio on the other, with an expansive fourteen-foot dining room table in between.

"What's so great about this house," says Julia, "is that the big floor-to-ceiling windows in the dining area make the garden feel part of the room. When you come in there's the living room and dining table and then the outdoors creates another room."

A small courtyard with a fountain directs the visitor to the front

PRECEDING PAGES: A concert grand piano provides a pedestal display for an Emmy, one of several won by Sorkin for his television show, *The West Wing.* RIGHT: Matching sofas facing a black-lacquered coffee table were custom made by the designer. A pair of club chairs found in an antiques store in Kansas were upholstered in the same fabric as the sofas. Steps terrace the room to the dining level.

door. Upon entering, you face the living room with a fireplace and chimney creating a divider to allow for an entrance hall on one side and a stairway leading to the private areas of the house on the other. A baby grand piano stands next to the stairs at the front of the room.

The furniture arrangement is classically symmetrical with matching custom sofas that face an oversized custom-made coffee table placed in front of the elegant limestone fireplace. A pair of custom-made leather ottomans sit directly in front of the hearth.

"I love the ottomans," says Julia, "which Martin made. As we traveled he really got to know what I loved and he made things for me if we couldn't find them."

Two large armchairs found by Lawrence in a shop in Kansas are upholstered in the same fabric as the sofas. The chairs, and a round table between them, provide a visual divider between the conversation grouping and the dining area a few steps away. A pair of console tables with round, butler-style mirrors hung above them were designed by Lawrence and are placed on either side of a doorway leading into a library/entertainment room.

"The best thing about this room is that it is great for entertaining," says Julia. "We've had wonderful parties here, the most memorable being the baby shower my friends threw for me before Roxy was born. When we have friends over and have cocktails in the seating area, no one wants to leave. It's so comfortable and convivial, especially when there is a fire and the front door is open and you can hear the fountain outside."

OPPOSITE: An English bull's-eye mirror over a console table is duplicated on both sides of the doorway leading to the entertainment viewing room.
LEFT: Julia Sorkin plays with her daughter, Roxy.

mid-century
classic

ROBIN AND MARC POLLACK take art, design, and the aesthetics of living quite seriously. She is a teacher, jewelry designer, ceramic artist, and devoted gardener. He is a gourmet cook, avid reader, and real-estate planner. The house they have restored together meshes their interest in thoughtful design and artistic integrity. It was built by one of the masters of mod-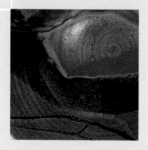ern architecture, Atlanta native Bill Finch, in the mid-1950s. Finch gained renown in the 1960s and '70s for his commercial designs. He designed the Coca-Cola and the Southern Bell headquarters, as well as numerous sports facilities, including the now defunct Atlanta–Fulton County Stadium. Before specializing in commercial architecture,

the Georgia Tech graduate and veteran of both World War II and the Korean War built residential structures with his then partner, Miller Barnes. It was one of these modernist jewels that the Pollacks chose to claim as their own.

Previous owners had done some reconstruction and added ornamentation to the inside and façade such as dental moldings and columns that presumably made the house fit with a more traditional, southern-style building vernacular. The Pollacks, recognizing the historical importance of their house, sought to restore its edgy modernism. Heriberto Brito, then working in Atlanta and considered one of the preeminent contemporary designers, assisted the Pollacks in reclaiming the artistic integrity of their home.

Indeed, Brito is committed to having his designs convey a sense of time and place. He also adheres to the tenets of organic architecture, understanding and heeding the felicitous relationship between indoor space and out, and integrating the natural features of a site into an overall design.

PRECEDING PAGES: A window wall creates a slender divide between indoors and out. In the corner, a ficus benjamina grows ceilingward, while its roots gather nutrients from outside beyond the wall. Antique Persian rugs help define the different areas in the expansive room. LEFT: The staircase and metal railings were designed by Brito. Classic mid-century modern furniture designs by Breuer, Corbusier, Eames, and Knoll inhabit the space. Banana flowers and protea provide an organic pop of color.

"What attracted us to the house was its classic, minimalist design," says Robin. "The open plan allows us to feel like we're a part of nature. It allows for a connection between our inside, daily activities with the outside, natural world."

Sited on a hill carefully planted with perennials and trees overlooking a five-acre lake, the Pollack house, constructed as it is with organic materials—brick, wood, slate, stone, marble, and glass—adds to the natural beauty of the setting.

A stone wall and lots of glass serve as a slender divider between outside and in. As in Frank Lloyd Wright's Usonian houses, the communal spaces—living/conversation area, dining space, and kitchen space—are open to each other with a fully glazed floor-to-ceiling "window wall." Doors in this wall open onto the patio, a terraced garden, and a path to a lakeside pavilion. To underscore the connection with nature, a large benjamin ficus tree, planted outside where its roots soak up rain, flourishes and grows ceilingward in the living room, with the glass wall built over the root.

The large, L-shaped living area is on the ground floor, reached by descending a floating wood and steel staircase from the front door. A conversation area faces a fireplace at one end of the room while the kitchen occupies the other. A dining area links the two spaces with numerous built-ins housing books and dishes along the way. In the L, seating faces a television/entertainment unit that is housed in a cabinet designed by Brito. A home office finishes off the space.

The furniture is a collection of who's who in mid-century design—Breuer, Knoll, Le Corbusier, Gehry—as well as new and custom pieces by local artists. SieMatic designed the kitchen that is outfitted as for a professional chef. Robin created many of the ceramic pieces and tableware.

The design and restoration of the house took about a year to complete. Robin, who does much of her pottery and jewelry design at home, felt frustrated that the construction phase prevented her from working at her art. That is, says Robin, "until I realized that I was doing art, just in a different form. I had Brito as my mentor and guide, fulfilling the saying that when the student is ready the teacher will appear. We believe that this home is now truly a reflection of our personality and values."

The house is now just as the Pollacks always imagined it could be. "We find the house peaceful—minimal but comfortable," continues Robin. "We can both work creatively here because the house, with its deference to light and space, beauty and nature, allows for the maximum flow of positive energy and inspiration."

OPPOSITE, LEFT: Robin sits in the
office area adjacent to the kitchen in
a Frank Gehry basket-weave chair.
OPPOSITE, RIGHT: A television
cabinet designed by Brito was made
by Ballacchino Design Custom
Furniture of Madagascar ebony. The
laminated maple plywood chair
and ottoman are by Michael Gilmartin.
ABOVE: The SieMatic designed
kitchen is professionally appointed
with a Viking stove and pastel
maple custom cabinetry. Robin's
hand-thrown pottery bowl graces
the granite countertop.

graphic
design

CONJURE UP THE IMAGE of a house in the country and the

home of Richard and Marcia Mishaan probably wouldn't be

what comes to mind. But in Sagaponack, New York, the

Mishaans have staked their claim on the agrarian landscape.

"Everybody's interpretation of country is different,"

explains Richard Mishaan, an interior designer and the owner

of Homer, an upscale home furnish-

ings store in Manhattan. "We started

out with a more traditional country

look and then it occurred to us, we

were much younger than the room was. Before we redid it, the liv-

ing room really didn't have much to do with us. We wanted to have

a room that more closely matched our design philosophy."

Their home and their living room in particular have become a glamorous yet functional blend of art, design, and technology. With each acquisition the room has evolved into a celebration of twentieth-century modern design showcasing the masters from Mies van der Rohe in the 1930s to Tommi Parzinger in the '50s.

"The pieces can stand alone," says Richard, "but the room came together so easily because they also look like they belong together. They have in common a clean, neutral elegance and together they make a strong design statement."

The setting for the Mishaan collection of furniture and art is a spacious home built in the early 1990s. The living room is light-filled and airy with a twelve-foot ceiling, four sets of French doors that lead into a sculpture garden situated behind the house, and a Louis XVI limestone fireplace surround that works remarkably well with the modern lines of the room's other pieces.

The Mishaans determined the room was complete when Richard found the Louise Nevelson sculpture that dominates one end of the oversized room. It fits as if it were made for the Mishaan house, its grid pattern mirroring the shapes of some of the other pieces in the room and even picking up the quirky lines in the rug, which Marcia designed as a modern take on a Tibetan tiger rug.

In the seating areas, matching sofas by Donghia upholstered in cream-colored mohair anchor both ends of the living room. In one grouping, the sofa faces a pair of 1940s French white leather-covered chairs with wing chairs at either end. In the other, love seats designed by Olivier Gagnère for Homer are upholstered in brown leather with linen-covered seats.

In case one is tempted to imagine that this living room is too rarified for the rigors of active country life, consider this: the Mishaan household includes two young children—Nicholas, a very rambunctious seven-year-old, and his equally energetic five-year-old sister, Alexandra—a Wheaton terrier named Spiky, and two Abyssinian cats. No room is off-limits to the younger Mishaans or their menagerie.

Modernism can look cold and stark. But juxtapose modern elements with African art, English architectural influences, and a glowing fire surrounded by old limestone, and you have a more humanized mix. Add to this children, pets, frequent guests, and lots of entertaining, and you have a space that is both stylish and hard-working—the embodiment of the new living room.

PRECEDING PAGES: A painted wood screen by Louise Nevelson provides a dramatic backdrop to the clean-lined furniture and other graphic elements in the room. The African sculptural pieces are from Homer, the sofa from Donghia. BELOW: Richard and Marcia play with Nicholas and Alexandra on the Donghia sofa. The pillow fabric was woven in Italy. OPPOSITE: A love seat by Olivier Gagnère for Homer. FOLLOWING PAGES: The walls are covered in a raw silk fabric from Cowtan & Tout. The glass occasional tables are vintage Mies van der Rohe designs. Brown leather and iron chairs designed by Eric Schmidt face the Nevelson sculpture. The rug was designed by Marcia.

The room celebrates modern design masters

from Mies van der Rohe to Tommi Parzinger.

penobscot
purview

REMEMBER THAT BOARD GAME, The Game of Life, found

at every getaway home with school-age children? Kids seem to

respond to this game because it answers, with the luck of a

draw, those questions that plague them as they ponder their

future—matters like what kind of job, salary, or house is likely

to come their way. For the young, board-game answers seem

just about as reasonable as anything

else. But imagine if adults, with one

lucky roll of the dice, could get the

chance to pick the card for "Dream

House"—a spacious, light, and airy retreat on the coast of Maine.

Can this really happen outside of board games? It can if you

happen to be the lucky winner in the HGTV Dream Home, an

event that captures the attention of thousands of hopeful players.

The HGTV Dream Home project pulls together a team—architects, builders, developers, interior and landscape designers—who work together to create a retreat that is specific to a coastal site. They solicit product manufacturers, furniture companies, and local artisans to contribute materials and talents to create and furnish a home that can withstand the heat, cold, wind, salt air, and humidity that are so challenging along the coast.

Douglas Govan, an architect for Acorn Homebuilders, designed this newly constructed home on the rugged Maine coast overlooking Penobscot Bay. The blueprint he came up with was a response to the panoramic vista offered from the site. Wanting to ensure water views from almost every room, he detailed a V-shaped design with wings extending from a point. The point, in this case, is the front door, which is set at a parallel line to the stretch of coastline that fronts the house.

Step through the front door and a spacious entrance gives way to the living room, a vaulted, two-story space that resonates with light and good cheer. Interior designer Linda Woodrum arranged the furniture groupings at angles to relate to different aspects and views in the room. A plump red sofa faces a gas fireplace set into a corner of the room and behind it, a long table is conveniently placed to relate to the dining table and to serve as a buffet or as a display area for cut flowers and books.

Nestled in the window nook are an elegantly draped table and two comfortable club chairs, making this the perfect spot for break-

PRECEDING PAGES: The vaulted ceiling and tall windows bring light and air into this room positioned to take full advantage of the incredible Penobscot Bay views. OPPOSITE: The Colette desk from the Chris Madden Collection for Bassett Furniture faces an antique leaded-glass windowpane suspended in the pass-through to the kitchen. RIGHT: A Lenox gas fireplace creates a cozy ambience in this four-season coastal home.

fast, afternoon tea, or an intimate dinner. A writing desk, its back to the kitchen, acts as a spatial divider but also makes an opportune spot to jot down a recipe.

The color scheme in the house employs a palette of neutrals and white against natural wood with one powerful exception. "I used red for its spontaneous burst of color," says Woodrum. "Red looks good in all seasons; it is a good foil against the occasional foggy, gray sky, and it offers a warm contrast with the blues of the sea, the greens in the ground cover, and the white of the birch trees. I also chose red because apples are abundant in this area of Maine and I wanted the color to relate to the environment as well."

Woodrum wanted to make sure that the lucky winner of the dream house would enter a home that was warm and inviting. She combed the antiques stores of the area for old farm signs, clamming baskets, quilts, and hooked rugs. She visited local artists to purchase works that were regional and specific to the area. She artfully arranged her finds throughout the home, on tables, hung from walls, and tucked into baskets, planting visual delights throughout the room.

If this is the dream house, are the dream job, salary, spouse, and children just around the corner? Perhaps they are for some lucky player in the real game of life.

RIGHT: Two Dorset chairs from the Chris Madden Collection for Bassett, covered in a neutral khaki, occupy a prominent position in the sunny corner. Pillows striped red and khaki add a splash of color, as does the tole lamp resting on the skirted table. An iron sculpture of a banded cow references the preferred local cattle. Sisal carpet is impervious to beach sand and damp shoes. An antique bench serves as a side table.

architectural
treasure

A YOUNG PROFESSIONAL couple with big-city jobs but suburban aspirations went house hunting one day along tree-lined streets in order to find a safe and roomy home in which to raise their son and daughter and a pair of outsized dogs. They envisioned Victorian, Dutch Colonial, Queen Anne, split-level, shingled saltbox, or stone bungalow. Realtor in tow, they stum-

bled through versions of each with a growing sense of dissatisfaction. And then, on a lark, they were shown a house so unexpected, so out-of-the-norm of the neighborhood, that they were jolted out of their ennui.

They dismissed it at first, but images of the house with its unadorned grace and spare simplicity haunted them. It spoke to

them in a language for which they hadn't yet learned the vocabulary, but still they listened. And then they bought. The couple, Jill and Mitch Rudnick, had discovered the charisma of Edward Durell Stone and their own modernist tendencies were unleashed.

"I had never really heard of him," says Jill, of the architect. "So it wasn't as if I was going out searching for one of his houses. But seeing the house for the first time as I did, even though the past owners did not decorate in a style particularly true to the architecture, still I saw something there . . . something that spoke to me very strongly."

"Stone is America's most misunderstood twentieth-century architect," says Jeffrey Bilhuber, the New York City designer who was hired to help interpret the architecture for the Rudnicks. "He is just now receiving a newfound respect for his craft and an awareness of his ability."

Edward Durell Stone is renowned for his International Style architecture. In this country, perhaps his most recognizable projects are the Museum of Modern Art and the Kennedy Center for the Performing Arts, but internationally he is known for, among other works, the U.S. embassy in New Delhi and the U.S. pavilion for the Brussels World's Fair, both finished in 1958. "For people who are lucky enough to own a Stone house, you become instant members of the E. D. S. fan

PRECEDING PAGES: A water table designed by Bilhuber is an example of materials that transcend their original purpose, with five-gallon jugs answering the question of where to put the flowers. RIGHT: The lowered ceiling at one end of the room provides more intimate spaces for dining above and a library and reading area below. A two-story window makes a glowing light wall in the midsection of the room, while the hearth end is more introspective without additional windows.

club," explains Bilhuber. "It's like a swap meet. These people get together and profess their undeclared love."

Bilhuber is now a fan. He realizes that he and Edward Durell Stone speak the same language of clarity. "I am not a spare modernist through any natural tendencies," explains Bilhuber. "Personally I'm more of an Anglophile and a collector. But I am attracted to modern design because of its clarity. It's just that until now, we haven't stepped far enough away from modernism for it to transcend time and become the classic which is its destiny."

The Rudnicks' living room has four main focal points. A chaise near the hearth offers cozy solitude. A stepped side table is an old piece that looks fresh in this context. "Jill inherited several pieces

Images of the house with its unadorned

grace and spare simplicity haunted them.

from her grandmother," says Bilhuber. "She couldn't imagine not using them in her new house. I sought to marry both—the old-fashioned sensibility with her newfound respect for modernity. And that ultimately is what makes this house look so modern. There is energy in the mixing which adds life and verve to both the old and the new."

In the conversation area, seating faces the expansive yard and garden. Here, a Bilhuber-designed "water table," made of eight five-gallon glass water bottles with a lacquered linen top, solves the dilemma of where to place the flowers. "You stick them right into the table," explains Bilhuber.

A dining/games area is a "divine size for children," declares Bilhuber. "The snowshoe chairs work well with the low Eero Saarinen table, making it the perfect spot for Emma and Zach, ages ten and twelve, and Jill and Mitch, to dine or play games together."

Underneath the dining-room overhang and in front of a picture window, a library nook offers an intimate spot for reading and conversation. The overhang creates a lowered ceiling, a more enclosed spot for the library. A few singular color blocks painted within the shelves echo the painted blocks on the walls near the fireplace and behind the sofa and the color-block effect of the area rugs, helping to define the different sections of the room. "Jill wanted to soften the 'big white box' characteristic of the architecture. We did so by adding the color blocks. Now color refers to the architecture and the geometry of the room, rather than dressing it. Paint was used as an application rather than an immersion."

Bilhuber is articulate in his speech and in his design. He knows what works and he knows how to meld his vision with his client's needs and desires, fitting them together in a coherent whole. Responding succinctly and honestly to vision and desire seems a design approach that Edward Durell Stone would have applauded. "I would like to believe that the architect is smiling down on us," says Jill. "That we have left the house with the energy, wisdom, and soothing calmness that is inherent in its soul."

PRECEDING PAGES: Jill inherited the serpentine dresser, circa 1940s, from her grandmother. An oversized French advertising poster leans on the floor. OPPOSITE: Color blocks of paint applied to the back of the bookshelves and to the walls in the room soften and warm a style that could resemble a big white box. Family pet Tucker happily ambles between the living room and garden through the glass doors in the middle of the room.

tuscan
inspiration

THE HOME of architect and designer James D'Auria and his wife, Jennifer, in Amagansett, New York, reflects the architect's passion for his craft. Recalls Jennifer, "The design of the house was entirely James's. He had several criteria. He wanted something barnlike, but with a modern edge. He also wanted the house to relate to the shingle-style architecture common to the Hamptons but not be traditional."

James D'Auria directs his own design firm, James D'Auria Associates, in New York City and has strong ties to the worlds of fashion, design, and retailing. He has designed showrooms and stores for Ellen Tracy, Joseph Abboud, and Guess?, among others. Jennifer is an actress who has made regular appearances

on *The Guiding Light* and is also chief financial officer of his firm.

On weekends, the D'Aurias head to their Long Island retreat. "We get to the house each weekend—we have to," Jennifer says. "If we didn't have that place to get away to, I'd go crazy. I grew up in the country in England in Herefordshire—near where Elizabeth Barrett Browning lived. It's very picturesque and I need to see the country and fields."

James D'Auria looks to Italy and, particularly, Tuscany, for his inspirations, both design and culinary. Their home, as Jennifer points out, "is infused with materials and elements found in Tuscan homes: red mahogany floors, stone patios, and different levels of landscaping."

The two-story living room—painted white—features floor-to-ceiling windows, which filter the famous Hamptons light through diaphanous white scrim curtains. Bookcases line both walls behind facing sofas framed in deep, dark mahogany and covered with white duck cushions and pillows. Black-and-white framed photographs are perched on the bookshelves on either side of the room.

PRECEDING PAGES: The light-filled study in the upper balcony over the living room is an inspiring place for James to work on design projects. Steel beams throughout mirror the traditional exposed wood beams of an Italian farmhouse design, though with a harder edge. OPPOSITE: A pair of Indonesian-inspired sofas and an African bench offer strong architectural lines softened by neutral fabrics and a sisal rug.

At one end of the living room, a balcony alcove houses D'Auria's office and study. Another D'Auria touch, construction beams on the ceiling, have been subtly finished and now house lighting on dimmers for the room. Two natural rush chairs are situated in front of each alcove. "We find this space inspiring," says Jennifer. "I think James is at his most creative when he's working here."

Discreet alcoves at the end of the living room under the overhanging office balcony hold a television set on one side and a storage unit for CDs and videos on the other. An elegant but casual bar is easily set up in the otherwise clean space.

"We love this room," says Jennifer. "At Christmas we get a huge tree to fill the room, and it's so much fun to have a place where there's plenty of room for everybody."

ABOVE: The nook beneath the office balcony overhang was an ideal spot for built-ins. Here the bookcase and cupboard create space for tapes and CDs, books, collectibles, and a bar service area. RIGHT: A clerestory swathes the room in light. James left many of the construction details exposed, such as the steel beams of the ceiling inset with lights. Bookcases running the length of the walls give the spare room a cozy library feel. Black-and-white photographs of architectural treasures from around the world line the top of the stacks.

IN LIVING COLOR

bohemian
rhapsody

MUCH HAS BEEN WRITTEN about the legendary Hollywood home of the late great director George Cukor, and about the man himself. Yet the current mistress of the manor is establishing herself as a legend in her own right. Lynn von Kersting is a world traveler—a seasonal ex-pat to Paris and Capri. She is a Renaissance woman—well read, schooled in languages, music, literature—and she brings this knowl-

edge to her design. Von Kersting owns Indigo Seas, a shop filled with the tastemaker's signature style in unique furniture, fabrics, and accessories. With her partner, Richard Irving, she also owns the noted restaurants The Ivy in Los Angeles and The Ivy at the Shore in Santa Monica. Yet despite her peripatetic

nature, her business ventures, and her immersion in Hollywood, one thing is strikingly clear about von Kersting: what is of utmost importance to her is her family, her friends, and her home.

Tucked away on a twisting, narrow lane high above Sunset Boulevard, the von Kersting–Irving home is hidden behind an ivy-covered wall. Enter the singular gate and the house emerges amid a mass of roses and fragrant shrubs. Inside, cozy, intimate arrangements of furniture and the comforting clutter of lives being lived—stacks of books, plentiful pillows, multiple floral arrangements, and swirling arrays of fabric—make it clear this is a home in use.

Von Kersting's living room is sensuous, exotic, worldly, and smart. The room easily gives itself to the time of the day—now an elegant breakfast spot, now a literary salon. For daughter India, the room is a place to do homework, practice voice exercises, or sprawl in front of a fire while her parents read comfortably nearby.

Von Kersting delights in the contrast of the home's old-world character and easy elegance with the bustle going on outside its walls. The living room is her haven. "It is so like the place that Henry James wrote about in the late eighteen-nineties while living in Venice in one of the grand palazzos," says Lynn. "What I love is that it has the same kind of couch in 'rosy dawn,' and 'medallions and arabesques of the ceiling.'" Indeed, the ceiling is a dazzle of delight with its elaborate cornices and details and the whole space is enveloped in a wash of light and color that is as much Venice as it is California.

The room is arranged in four distinct groupings. At one end, nineteenth-century Chinese jars are arranged on an eighteenth-

PRECEDING PAGES: The floor-to-ceiling bay window blurs the line between outdoors and indoors, giving this area of the room the feel of a solarium. Intense color lends the room an extra glow. LEFT: Behind the sofa, blue-and-white vases stand on an eighteenth-century Chinese lacquer chest. A painted leather chinoiserie screen stands in the corner.

century lacquered armoire. Paintings and other objets d'art are abundantly displayed on the back wall. In the area in front of the hearth, a comfortable sofa, extra-long daybed/chaise, floor cushions, and an upholstered bench overlaid with a nineteenth-century paisley shawl provide relaxed seating.

A pedestal table, loosely draped in an antique sari, is the centerpiece for a dining arrangement in front of a mullioned window nook. At the other end of the room, another conversation grouping sits in a sunny niche.

Bringing her great sense of style to her living room, house, and gardens, von Kersting is aware that she is also preserving a piece of Hollywood history. She consciously saved fragments left over from the great decorator Billy Haines when he originally designed the house for George Cukor. Famous for his generosity, Cukor hosted some of Hollywood's most memorable characters, including Katharine Hepburn, the Barrymores, Vivien Leigh, and the Selznicks. Von Kersting is also famously generous, sharing with family and friends her grace, humor, and exceptional home.

ABOVE: A papier-mâché tray with a collection of antique dice sits on a first-edition Cecil Beaton book. LEFT: A sofa transforms this sunny bay area into a library corner. Eighteenth- and nineteenth-century fabrics from France, China, and India vie for attention with the brilliantly colored roses from the surrounding gardens. OPPOSITE: A collection of lacquered Indian and chinoiserie boxes stands on an eighteenth-century Moorish chest. The architectural integrity of the room was maintained, but the walls and ceiling were painted a deep Moorish red.

cabana
color

WHEN A WELL-TRAVELED, design-savvy Atlanta couple turned to designer John Oetgen and asked him to transform their 1970s-modern South Carolina beach home into a whimsical, carefree house, they found the right guy. Oetgen knows how to have fun and he tickled just the right bone in this living room.

"I wanted the room to have lots of personality," says Oetgen of the year-round getaway house for the couple, their grown children, and several grandchildren.

The family area of the house, combining the living and dining rooms and the kitchen, is on the second floor up a curving stairway, to better take advantage of the scenic water views. When one arrives at the top of the stairs, the effect is one of brilliant light, color, and angles, with a distinct sense of playfulness very carefully orchestrated.

"First and foremost, I wanted the room to appeal to the eyeballs," Oetgen says. "The original house took itself way too seriously to be on the beach. I opened up the space and applied angles, spoofing the original architecture."

Not satisfied with just that ploy, Oetgen layered on the color. "The color was a bit of a stretch for my clients. They were used to minimalism, white walls to showcase their serious collection of modern art. I introduced cool summer hues—lavender, plum, pale mist, and other shades of blue and green—and applied them in unexpected places."

In one of Oetgen's boldest strokes, an actual beach cabana houses a television and electronic accessories. The graphic black-and-white awning stripes of the cabana and sofa pop against red Saarinen bucket chairs in this media seating area. In the space designated for yet more fun and games, a card table and chairs stand at the ready. The games table is demurely hidden behind a dividing wall painted a lush sea green. Step around the corner to find a child-friendly "time-out" space, with a chaise poised for contemplation and relaxation. All of the individual areas are defined, floating on their own round islands of white shag carpeting. "I wanted the shag islands to rest on floors stained an aquamarine, but that was really pushing it," Oetgen explains.

A dining table roomy enough to seat the whole gang angles toward the kitchen and the dividing island that signals you've arrived at the land of snacks. The family is celebrated in a wall of black-and-white head-shots. The wall has a few blank spaces for expected new members, though a number of children are already featured in the op-art arrangement of the photos.

"The house was totally deconstructed for relaxation and fun," says Oetgen. "The living room especially was designed for bare feet, barely-there attire, and real beach attitude."

PRECEDING PAGES: Round shag rugs suggest individual islands that define and unify the different areas of the living room. BELOW: A wall of photographs behind the dining table lets every family member star. The room opens up to the kitchen on the right. The Knoll table is surrounded by Donghia chairs. OPPOSITE: The wash of applied color adds motion and fluidity to the room and makes the black-and-white touches pop.

new england
tradition

WHEN YOUR DECORATOR becomes your best friend,

a happy collaboration is the result. Your project ceases to be

seen as a chore or as a task to be completed on a prescribed

decorator/client schedule. Rather, ideas and their implementa-

tion are allowed to evolve over coffee and joint shopping ven-

tures. The space matures with the relationship and is never

caught in the decorator time warp,

forever dated to the month and year

it was finally "finished."

Kathy and Jack Haire's house in

Rowayton, Connecticut, is a stone, slate, and stucco beauty. Fraser

Peters, the designer and builder, established his reputation in the

early 1920s, constructing similarly designed homes in the coastal

towns and hamlets of New England. This house is U-shaped, with the main entrance and large living room occupying the center and the kitchen, the garage, and the bedrooms in the wings.

The Haires were delighted to find the house in 1993 when they returned to New England from Chicago. They moved in on December twentieth, with their two small boys, Billy, then a first-grader, and John, in preschool. "It was a terrible time to move, just days before Christmas," remembers Kathy. "The house had been rented for fifteen years before we bought it. It was in pretty bad shape. Still, we put up a tree and lit the fire and it was magical."

Fortunately, Kathy had already enlisted Roxie Hennemuth to help make their new purchase into a home. "Roxie and I had worked on houses together before," says Kathy. "We have become great friends as we've worked together over a dozen years and on four houses."

Kathy and Roxie didn't make any architectural changes to the living room. Its soaring ceiling, glass doors that open to the gardens, and oversized fireplace were all original. They did add emphasis to the fireplace wall by replacing a single, slab mantel with a custom, carved-pine surround built by Dave Bartlett and faux-painted by Sherry Ringler to look like mahogany. They also decided to paint the room a deep, rich, oxblood red.

PRECEDING PAGES: The family's yellow lab, Herrigan, snoozes in the afternoon sunshine. The television is housed in a nineteenth-century French armoire. The club chair is upholstered in a Ralph Lauren paisley. LEFT: A cheerful yellow entry opens up to an oxblood-red room. The white-painted beamed ceiling reflects the light down onto bare wood floors, making the room look as if it's glowing. Sofa fabric is Cowtan & Tout.

"I wanted red," says Kathy. "It is a big room so I wanted to paint it a color that would cozy it up and add warmth. I chose the oxblood color because I wanted it to have some brown in it. It eventually became a custom color after much trial and error because I needed to make it just right for the room."

In contrast, the once-dark ceiling was painted a creamy white, lifting it up visually. The space now has the enveloping intimacy of an interior room such as a library, but with the cheerful, sunlit sparkle of a room that opens to the garden and soars to the rafters.

The room is visually divided into four areas. An entrance hall, painted a welcoming warm yellow, showcases a collection of brown-transferware plates and helps mark the transition from entrance to living room. A stately grand piano is placed just inside the living room. In the center, a pedestal table offers a cozy dining spot in winter and a library table in summer, with stacks of books and vases of flowers. The chairs are removed to open up the area and let sunlight bathe the bare floors.

A writing table juts into the seating area and doubles as an end table. Two comfortable sofas provide an intimate conversation area near the large hearth. An armoire holds a television and entertainment equipment.

The windows are left unadorned year round. The decorating team considered window treatments, but the living room is granted privacy through the house's U-shaped design. The views offered from the living room include colorful border gardens, a large stone patio, and a tidal pond, a favorite spot for many types of saltwater fowl. "We have the doors open all summer," says Kathy. "The room is so peaceful and romantic with the garden just outside the door and the water so close to the house."

In a living room at once cozy and spacious, enveloping and expansive, the Haires have found the perfect balance between public room and intimate family gathering space. Yet it is never finished. It remains a canvas ready for reinvention and interpretation, where items can come and go according to the seasons, furniture can be rearranged to suit different occasions, and a friendship based on design and collecting can continue to flourish.

OPPOSITE, LEFT: Cosmopolitans are served on a nineteenth-century tole tray atop a Cowan & Tout–upholstered bench. OPPOSITE, RIGHT: A nineteenth-century English bamboo cabinet holds antique silver pieces. Brown-and-white transferware is a favorite collectible. ABOVE: Windows open like doors to allow easy access to the garden. A central table holds stacks of books in summer and is an elegant place to dine near the hearth in winter.

persian palette

A GREAT APPRECIATION of Islamic culture is everywhere apparent at the home of Nancy and Buddy Moss of San Marino, California. As she traveled to Iran, Morocco, Somalia, Turkey, and Egypt with her husband, a specialist in the building of wells in dry places, Nancy became mesmerized by the exotic life of the desert that finds expression in brilliant color, lush textiles, and intricate patterns.

"I am a collector," she says. "After several trips to Iran I became a great fan of that part of the world. I brought home fabrics, rugs, and other objects. I was confident that I could put together what I loved and make it work." But Nancy, a clinical psychologist with a private practice, found herself unable to decide how best to incorporate all her collections in her home. It was then that fate intervened. Dyala Salam, an antiques dealer in London specializing in Islamic textiles and artifacts, was instrumental in bringing together Kate Stamps and another customer of his, Nancy Moss.

"I knew of Kate Stamps, followed her work at various show houses and in magazines, but it wasn't until I found out that Kate and I purchased from the same London dealer that I arranged to meet with her company," explains Nancy.

Meeting Kate and Odum Stamps, partners in the Pasadena architecture and design firm Stamps & Stamps, turned out to be very favorable for the Mosses. Kate is a garden and interior designer while her husband Odum is an architect. "They share my enthusiasm for Islamic design and understood my vision," says Nancy.

Another person on the design team particularly sensitive to Islamic art and architecture was Laurel Myers, a designer with Kate Stamps. "We met with Nancy and became attuned to how she wanted to incorporate her extensive collection of textiles with the way she and Buddy actually live," says Laurel. "We encouraged her to consider a more European fantasy of Islamic style rather than a pure and literal translation to meet their needs for comfort and family togetherness." In other words, Buddy could live with a sixteen-foot built-in banquette but he wouldn't abandon his easy chair.

The Moss home was originally built in 1926 in a style that was popular in California at the time, a blending of Spanish Colonial and Mission bungalow. The renovation involved more of a reinterpretation of the architecture than a reconstruction of it. For instance, the raised ceiling, exposed rafters, built-in bookshelves, doorways, and raised seating niche were original to the house. But Stamps & Stamps reinterpreted these details. They added barrel arches between the ceiling beams, intricately carved built-ins of plaster rather than wood with cornices of Islamic design above them, antique columns to demarcate the seating niche, and portières in the doorways fashioned from antique *souzannis,* or "wedding drapery" fabric panels purchased in Iran and Uzbekistan.

The living-room area is one large room that extends from the

PRECEDING PAGES: A pelmet found in Morocco and hung in the doorway was one of the original pieces of inspiration for the room's décor. OPPOSITE: A fine eighteenth-century Isphahan carpet sets the tone for the elegance of the room. A chandelier from Indigo Seas mirrors the pair of French lusters on the mantel. Coral beads and shells provide natural color. One of a pair of eighteenth-century chairs is upholstered in Raphael Damask by Scalamandré.

ABOVE: The reverse side of the pelmet frames the view at the other end of the long living room, where French doors lead out to a protected terrace and a sunny dining spot. The pelmet shape echoes the ceiling and the carved niches of the bookcases. A banquette runs along the wall, with built-in bookcases overhead. OPPOSITE: A contemplative niche with banquette is built on an elevated platform opposite the fireplace.

front of the house to the covered portico at the back, about a fifty-foot-long space, twenty feet wide. While it is typical of California living to include an outdoor area as part of the main living space, Nancy chose to concentrate on creating an interior feel.

"I like dark interior rooms," explains Nancy. "Being in southern California you already get plenty of sun so I wanted a cozy space."

Color became a major design element, and the large seventeenth-century Persian carpet in the formal seating area helped determine the colors for the rest of the room—plum, salmon, maroon, and gold. The walls are not painted; rather the color was mixed into the plaster in a Venetian technique called *galice.* Each layer applied is a different color, which is then burnished and waxed to give the walls the luster of ancient stucco. A stenciled raised relief of plaster was the finishing touch, further embellishing and emphasizing the Islamic design motif.

The biggest challenge was dividing the large space to create defined areas for formal seating, casual entertainment, dining, and reading, with an arrangement conducive to traffic flow. The banquette seating in both the entertainment space and the formal seating area is a European translation of Moroccan banquettes and has the advantage of providing seating for large gatherings while not restricting the smooth flow of people throughout the different areas. The U-shaped banquette area on the raised platform is both romantic and intimate.

Ultimately, Nancy and her collaborators at Stamps & Stamps created a room that celebrates myriad design influences and, most important, a space where Nancy and Buddy could satisfy their goal of living comfortably, with a generous and stylish space to entertain their friends, children, and grandchildren.

"I am a secret perfectionist," confesses Nancy. "As a psychologist, I suppose I could identify my love of collecting as an addiction. But it brings us both joy, especially when we can live surrounded by the things that give us such pleasure, imbued as they are with history and culture."

industrial
chic

RICHARD AND LISA BAKER sited their new home on what
was once an expansive eighteenth-century farm in southern
New England, blessed with undulating hills and natural out-
croppings of rock. Vestigial stone fencing, piled long ago in an
effort to clear the fields and demarcate the land, is still in evi-
dence. Deer, wild turkey, and many types of small, furry ani-

mals are also abundant. Here, next to
a polo field and sequestered from the
more mundane aspects of suburban
life, the Bakers found a perfect spot to
build a home in the grand tradition of an English country manor.

Interior designer Karen Houghton worked with architect Rick

Moisan to help the Bakers realize their dream. "The Bakers had a

very strong sense of what they wanted the house to be," says Houghton. "While it didn't necessarily translate to specific details, they wanted an English-country-house look that was accommodating to their three young children. They also wanted a house that was casual but with enough formal rooms to entertain a broad range of people in them."

The design plan for the interior was inspired by a trip to England. "Together we went on a buying trip to London," recalls Houghton. "We bought the two George Smith sofas as well as a behind-the-sofa table. We really had to search for the dining table and chairs because we wanted an English country table but it needed to be narrow to fit the space. We finally found that in England, as well."

Ample windows line both sides of the large living room. French doors lead to a courtyard patio by the dining table, and Dutch doors open onto formal gardens on the other side of the room.

This casual living space encompasses a kitchen, built-in desk/ storage area, dining table, conversation area, and a fireplace flanked by built-ins that house toys and games on the left and television and entertainment equipment on the right.

The table, situated on a slant, leads the eye from the kitchen into the conversation and entertainment seating area. The sofas were made more casual by mixing their upholstery fabric: plaid for the seat cushions and a solid cranberry fabric for the rest. An upholstered swivel chair is a favorite spot for the children to perch on as it easily turns from the conversation area to the television for viewing.

PRECEDING PAGES: Factory cogs and glove forms make an industrial statement. The top of the tufted leather ottoman lifts off for extra storage. A pair of George Smith sofas provide seating. LEFT: A nineteenth-century English farmhouse table provides a visual link between the kitchen and seating area, while the angle draws you into the room. The white vaulted ceiling hung with industrial lighting fixtures helps keep the room bright and sunny.

"This room doesn't take the English look too far," says Houghton. "But it does have some signature marks—the color of the cabinets, for instance, and the choice of playful, casual upholstery for the sofas and pillows. I think the room feels very friendly."

A leather ottoman serves as both coffee table and a place to put your feet up. It was custom made with a large storage area underneath the hinged top, "for all the odd bits and toys that you don't know what to do with," says Houghton.

The American style in the room is most noticeable in the collection of objects once used either for work or play. Old toys—an antique pickup and tractor, an old Bingo numbers tosser, and toy cannons—add visual interest for adults and children alike. "Lisa picked up the weighted pins that are arranged on the storage units. They were widely used in the early 1900s as exercise equipment. People used them as weights, to hold while bending and stretching. They also became favorite juggling tools," says Houghton.

In contrast to the playthings, old molds from now defunct factories pay homage to an industrial America. Le Corbusier once said that a house is a machine for living. In this living room, wooden gears from a turn-of-the-century factory in Pennsylvania artfully arranged on the native fieldstone fireplace serve as reminders of that fact. Like gears in motion, this space is perfectly suited for the task at hand, a gathering spot for a busy family of five, equipped so they can all meet on equal ground.

OPPOSITE, LEFT: Built-in cupboards keep children's toys and games tidy. Toy cannons and pins go on top.
OPPOSITE, CENTER: An antique milk bottle carrier holds magazines.
OPPOSITE, RIGHT: Red buckets, one for each child, help keep order in the office area. ABOVE: A view to the kitchen, where an extended island provides casual dining space and plenty of work surface. Suspended pots echo the industrial feel, as does the stainless expanse of refrigeration.

LIVING IN THE PAST

camp little
pine

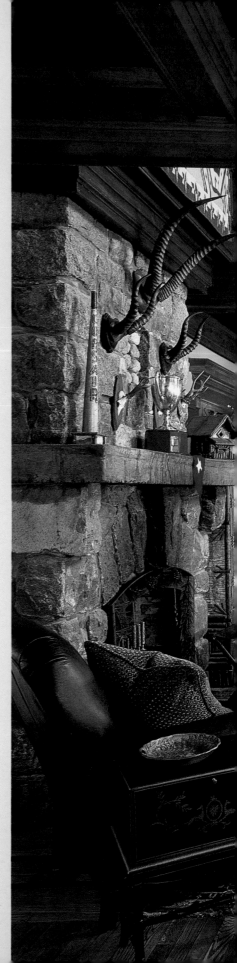

DURING THE GILDED AGE of the late nineteenth century, privileged families escaped from the city heat by building summer estates in remote spots along the sea or lakeshore, in the woods or mountains of the Northeast. In the Adirondack region of upstate New York, some of America's wealthiest families acquired vast properties on which they built "great camps."

Michael Bird, an architect in Lake Placid, New York, spent summers at one such estate, Camp High Pines, which belonged to his grandparents. Camp High Pines, situated on the shores of Upper Saint Regis, comprises numerous buildings and dwellings of the traditional great camp: a main house, a boat house, several guest houses, and

work buildings. Perhaps in response to this early exposure, Michael became an architect, and his firm, Adirondack Design Associates, specializes in the modern interpretation of the great camp.

Several years ago, when Michael was still dating his wife, Mari Kirwood, an interior designer, he introduced her to the pleasures of life in the Adirondacks. "I arrived as a lunch guest and I never left," says Mari. "I took to it instantly. There was so much to love about the Adirondacks. I learned about the beauty of the architecture through Michael and I adapted the style to my own design."

When Bird and Kirwood married, Bird's family presented him with a quirky old 1900s cottage that was once the "starter's shack" for the golf club that surrounds their property. "It was pretty much the same footprint of the house you see now," says Michael. "The house was surrounded by porches, which we converted to bedrooms and baths. We enclosed the back porch and made it an extension of the living room."

The materials used in the renovation of the house are all local: poplar, cedar, white birch, and fieldstone. A large fieldstone fireplace dominates the living room. A center vault ceiling visually enlarges the space and provides natural light through an upper clerestory. The addition of a balcony railing in the vaulted area provides display space for the Birds' collection of Navajo rugs. "The vaulted ceiling and fireplace are original," says Bird. "We added the birch bark. Birch trees are almost synonymous with the Adirondacks, so using the peeled bark as a wall cover relates to the environment but it also lightens the space with the almost white, reflective surface of the bark." Birch-bark paneling extends out to the porch, connecting it to the interior and the exterior; birch trees are also used as support pillars on the porch.

The Birds moved into their newly renovated home in August 2001, just after the birth of their baby, Hunter, that July. And what will Hunter have to look forward to? "The peacefulness of summers in the Adirondack park," says Mari, is what makes the Adirondacks so special to the generations of families who spend time there.

ABOVE: A local craftsman made the console table behind the sofa. The boat model is a reminder of a favorite summer activity. Another tête-à-tête seating area is behind the sofa. OPPOSITE, LEFT: Birch paneling on the walls of the porch are used on the exterior as well as the interior vaulted ceiling. OPPOSITE, RIGHT: Mari with her son, Hunter, at the games table in the room. French doors beyond open to the summer porch.

Four seasons of recreation make

the Adirondack park so inviting.

family
ties

UNUSUAL IN THIS DAY of transient housing, the McDermott

family home in Rye, New York, is now occupied by its fourth

generation. If a living room is a place where, as the well-worn

proverb goes, "families who play together stay together," then

the McDermott living room is the great-granddaddy of them

all. Though the neighborhood has changed from what was

once rolling farmland, the house itself

appears to have been untouched by

time. Yet it seems perfectly adapted

for modern living, suitable for a busy

family with three school-age children and a dog. It is rich in family

memories, heirlooms, recycled castoffs, and collections—in other

words, rich in the stuff of lives lived to the fullest.

Becky McDermott is a decorator who inherited the house after the death of her parents. When she was first starting out in the design trade and living nearby, her mother asked her to redo the living room—or, in family parlance, the back room—so it could more easily accommodate the growing extended family. Interestingly, at the turn of the nineteenth century, the McDermott home served as the men's clubhouse for the legendary Apawamis Club; the living room was originally the men's locker room. When the clubhouse was moved and the building was converted to family dwellings, bookshelves were installed where lockers once stood. Years later, Becky painted the backs of those shelves in soft olive chosen to accentuate her outstanding collection of Nantucket baskets.

"That collection began on my twenty-first birthday," says Becky. "We had vacationed in Nantucket for many years and my parents gave me this little Nantucket basket and inside it was an emerald ring." This basket became the first of many and the focal point of a room.

For her parents, Becky created three separate areas in the living room according to their specifications. These included an area for conversation and music in front of the hearth, an antique card table that also doubles as a library table, and a bar area tucked in the back of the room. Princeton roots run deep in the family, so Becky's mother replaced the original game board, hidden underneath the card table's solid top, with a backgammon board that she needlepointed in the school's traditional orange and black.

When Becky, with her husband, Tom, three kids, and dog,

PRECEDING PAGES: Slip-covered sofas, neutral upholstery, and sisal carpet work well with the Jane Churchill geometric floral Roman shades. RIGHT: A games area at the back of the room doubles as a library table, useful when perusing the extensive collection of books that has grown with each successive generation. A weathered porch column purchased on Nantucket serves as a plant stand.

ABOVE: An heirloom blue-and-white export porcelain pitcher adds a punch of color to the shelves. A simple mantel display offers calming visual relief. OPPOSITE, LEFT: The older McDermott kids, Ted and Betsy, relax in the back room. OPPOSITE, RIGHT: A game board, needlepointed in Princeton colors, is revealed under the antique tabletop.

moved back into the house in 1997, she explains, "I needed to change the room after the death of my parents."

Becky chose to do so in calming neutrals. She selected a wool sisal rug to cover the hardwood floors and painted the stuccoed walls white. She reupholstered Tom's favorite chair and ottoman in raisin-colored chenille, and slipcovered flea-market furniture finds in a unifying washable, kid- and dog-friendly white cotton duck.

The bookshelves house generations of cherished volumes, 1,200 or so in all. "Many are first editions or are of historical interest, on the Dutch influence in the area and the Civil War, or sets of encyclopedias," explains Becky.

The 1960s-era television set wasn't there when her parents were alive. "That was a concession to my children, who enjoy watching Yankees games and movies here," says Becky.

Other pieces in the room reflect family interests and travels. The pine columns are from a porch in Nantucket, the mirror on the mantel was from an upstairs room, and the prints on the wall were taken from an old book of architectural drawings.

Can a house with eighteenth-century roots really be an example of the new American living room? It can if that room has always been the place where the family gathered to read, eat, drink, be entertained, and play together. Or if it is, as Becky describes it, "the heart of the home," as it has been for many generations.

past
perfect

APRIL IN NEW YORK is expressed in abundant sprays of forsythia spilling out of the boundaries of Central Park, daffodils marching up Park Avenue, and the Kips Bay Boys and Girls Club Decorator Showhouse, or, to those in the know, simply "Kips Bay." It is here, working without clients or budget constraints, that designers can let their imaginations run

free. In the 1998 showhouse, designer Bunny Williams designed a living room/salon that not only stood the test of time, it transcended it. For the catalogue, she titled her room "Past and Present."

At first glance, the look and feel of the room is nineteenth-century fin-de-siècle, but look closely, and it encompasses the turn

The room is marked by eclecticism, material

OPPOSITE: An eighteenth-century secretary is paired with a twentieth-century steel and stretched hide sculptural chair. ABOVE: Celadon vases line up along the mantel, each with a single elephant ear frond. Paintings are hung to the ceiling, in a diversity of genre, period, and subject matter.

comfort, and and an appreciation of design.

archival
ambience

THE CLIENT SAID they needed a comfortable living room for a family of five—a place where the children could cuddle up with a parent to read or watch television, the adults could work at the computer or pay bills, where an evening might be given over to a game of cards or friends might step in for cocktails. Then, they also wanted space for more than 3,000 books and a museum-quality collection of vintage baseball cards, scorecards, and stacks of newspaper clippings documenting historic ball games since the turn of the twentieth century. It was only natural for a designer to think "library."

Penny Drue Baird, of the New York design firm Dessins, came

up with an ingenious plan to oblige her client and his passion for books and sports memorabilia. "The shape of the room was a challenge," concedes Baird. "Besides the books and an extensive collection of baseball artifacts and memorabilia, the clients brought with them some rather large pieces to try and make 'fit' in the narrow, L-shaped space. I needed to accommodate a large partners desk, numerous file cabinets, a hexagonal games table and six chairs, and glass-fronted library cases."

The ceiling height varies throughout the room because one portion of the room is tucked underneath the second floor of the house while the main part of the library is two-storied with a partial balcony. The ceiling variations alternately provide spaces of intimacy and openness. In the area in front of the fireplace, the ceiling is dropped and wall-to-ceiling paneling helps create a coziness appropriate for a comfortable sofa, numerous club chairs, and an oversized upholstered ottoman begging for occupants to put their feet up. A television stationed in a recessed alcove beside the hearth offers another reason to turn and gaze in that direction. Behind the sofa, the long portion of the L makes the bend and extends to a gracious pair of French doors leading to the gardens beyond.

In the main library room, a partner's desk and the necessary office accoutrements anchor one end of the space. At the other, the games table stands at the ready. Between these spaces is another sofa, purchased in England of tufted leather, and a large table that serves for coffee, cocktails, or reference material.

To adequately house the volumes of books, the vellum-bound

PRECEDING PAGES: A tufted leather sofa and a pair of club chairs provide comfortable seating in the library. A hexagonal card table is set for poker night. Antique light fixtures and a spiral staircase from Paris add a patina of age to the new room. RIGHT: An upholstered ottoman invites one to perch or put the feet up; the glass top in the center provides a level spot for flowers and beverages. Stark carpeting runs throughout.

ABOVE: In this section of the library the lowered ceiling creates greater intimacy. A comfortable sofa faces both fireplace and corner television. OPPOSITE, LEFT: Babe Ruth artifacts—a signed letter and an original black-and-white photograph—are examples of the library's fine collection of sports memorabilia. OPPOSITE, RIGHT: Glass-fronted library cases holding first-edition books line the balcony at the top of the circular stair.

newspaper clippings, and the sports-related artifacts such as a photo album of Babe Ruth and the New York Giants in Japan, the library extends to a three-sided balcony on one end of the room. The client's own law-library cases were built in on this second floor, with the glass-fronted cases offering protection for the rare documents. A nineteenth-century circular staircase connects the lower and upper library stacks. "It was purchased in one of the flea markets in Paris," explains Baird. "It was disassembled bit by bit, shipped to New York, and reconstructed in a workshop in Greenwich, Connecticut."

Antique lighting fixtures, mahogany stained paneling, iron balustrades, and antique carpet runners add to the patina of the library, which was, in fact, newly constructed in 2001.

"My clients wanted this room to house a valuable collection yet serve many other functions with style and grace. I think this room's strength lies in making a successful marriage between the raw space and what goes well in it—in merging the client's own look, passions, and sense of style with the requirements for the room."

With the astounding collection of books, vintage photo albums, letters, score cards, first editions, and other memorabilia, one could be comfortably immersed in this room for a very long time.

beaux arts
classic

THE TURN-OF-THE-CENTURY Beaux Arts architectural

style in America—with its European, particularly French, roots

and influence—was a style usually reserved for lofty institu-

tions and monumental public buildings. In New York City,

structures such as the Woolworth Building and Grand Central

Station are fine examples of the formality and symmetry char-

acterized by Beaux Arts. It was also

adopted by a few late-nineteenth- and

early-twentieth-century business mag-

nates and robber barons for mansions

befitting their new status and wealth. It is not, however, an archi-

tectural style one might expect to find as an example of the new

American living room. But enter Landmark Restoration, a Los

Angeles firm whose mission is to "appropriately update older houses to fit the needs of modern living while maintaining the integrity of the original structure." The company's principal partners, Tim Corrigan and Kathleen Scheinfeld, have restored and updated a legendary Los Angeles mansion and made it their own. Their living room is steeped in the history and grandeur of the American Renaissance period that gave rise to the Beaux Arts style, yet it is light, airy, comfortable, and completely modern.

Like most mansions, this one comes with a pedigree. Corrigan and Scheinfeld purchased the house from the estate of Dorothy Chandler, philanthropist, cultural icon, and the wife of the publisher of the *Los Angeles Times*, Norman Chandler. It was Dorothy Chandler who did so much to promote culture and the arts in her city from the 1950s until her death in the late 1990s. With her husband she raised funds to build the Los Angeles Music Center, and for many years the annual Academy Awards ceremony was held in the Dorothy Chandler Pavilion.

PRECEDING PAGES: Oversized, slip-covered, custom-designed furniture adds a carefree American touch to the rest of the room's elegant neoclassical details, which include an eighteenth-century Italian chandelier, Chinese coral, and ancient statuary. LEFT: *Faux-marbre* Corinthian columns behind nineteenth-century French side tables from Sotheby's share space with a modern glass and steel coffee table, lightening the mood in this gardenside living room. The balloon shades are made up from Scalamandré fabric.

The home was built in 1913, designed by J. Martyn Haenke and W. J. Dodd and commissioned by Dr. Peter Janss, a real-estate tycoon who helped develop Westwood and the Holmby Hills sections of the growing city. Corrigan and Scheinfeld jumped at the opportunity to buy the home in 1997, without even a walk-through.

"We were thrilled with the purchase," says Scheinfeld, "but we didn't really have any idea of the amount of renovation it would take to restore and update this home for modern living. Even though Dorothy Chandler lived here until her death in 1997, for the last decade of her life she didn't really use any of it except her bedroom suite. The servants sent meals up to her from the kitchen in the dumbwaiter. The rest of the rooms really deteriorated."

Public rooms on the ground floor of the mansion include a grand foyer with an elegantly paneled dining room on one side and a "gentleman's study" on the other. The casual living room stands as a bridge between a more formal, Venetian-inspired library salon and the expansive kitchen at the back of the house. It looks out onto a lap pool, surrounded by manicured shrubbery and flower gardens. "The Chandlers did so much entertaining in the early years that the backyard was paved over as a parking lot," says Scheinfeld. "It took three months to jackhammer out the concrete that was poured three feet deep. We completely relandscaped with more than three hundred trees and rosebushes."

The challenge that Corrigan faced in renovating the interiors was to maintain the integrity of the house but to give the rooms a relaxed quality, making them cleaner, lighter, and more contemporary in feeling. "The walls in this room were gray travertine marble," explains Scheinfeld. "They seemed cold and unfriendly. Tim had the walls sandblasted, scored, and stained to resemble blocks of French limestone." Sea-grass carpeting over stately terrazzo floors is the perfect foil for their formality.

As Dorothy Chandler supported the arts and culture in Los Angeles, so do Corrigan and Scheinfeld continue her tradition in their home and business. They periodically open their home to cultural groups and fund-raising events promoting music and the arts. In their loving restoration of a historic Beaux Arts residence, they have ensured its preservation yet reinterpreted its vernacular for a new generation seeking to fuse the historic past with the modern present.

RIGHT: A painting by Carolus-Duran presides over a marble console table holding an array of objects, including a lamp fashioned from a marble sculpture.
OPPOSITE: Winston the Westie enjoys a comfortable perch on a nineteenth-century salon chair. A wood urn mold sits In front of the open French doors leading to the pool and gardens.

Acorn Homebuilders
Douglas Govan, Architect
(800) 727-3325
www.acorns.com

Adirondack Design Associates
77 Riverside Drive
Saranac Lake, NY 12983
(518) 891-5224

Penny Drue Baird
787 Madison Avenue, Third Floor
New York, NY 10021
(212) 288-3600

Bruce Bierman Design Inc.
29 West 15th Street
New York, NY 10011
(212) 243-1935

Jeffrey Bilhuber, Inc.
330 East 59th Street
New York, NY 10022
(212) 308-4888

Heriberto J. Brito ASID
BRITO LLC
3400 SW 27th Avenue
Miami, FL 33133
(305) 858-4090

James D'Auria Associates
20 West 36th Street, Twelfth Floor
New York, NY 10018
(212) 268-1142

Pam Duncan
Wiseman & Gale & Duncan
Interiors, Inc.
150 S. Saint Francis Drive
Santa Fe, NM 87501
(505) 984-8544

Susan DuPépé Interior Design, Inc.
220 McKenzie Street
Santa Fe, NM 87501
(505) 982-4536

Julia Durney Interiors, Ltd.
79 Putnam Park Road
Bethel, CT 06801
(203) 798-7110

Mark P. Finlay Architects, AIA
1300 Post Road, Suite 101
Fairfield, CT 06430
(203) 254-2388

William Hodgins, Inc.
232 Clarendon Street
Boston, MA 02116
(617) 262-9541

Karen Houghton Interiors
41 North Broadway
Nyack, NY 10960
(914) 358-0133

Mari Kirwood Design Associates
3 Garden Street
Rhinebeck, NY 12572
(845) 876-4848

Landmark Restoration
455 Lorraine Blvd.
Los Angeles, CA 90020
(323) 525-1805

Martynus, Inc.
616 N. Almont Drive
West Hollywood, CA 90069
(310) 385-8730

Becky McDermott Interiors
Hidden Spring Lane
Rye, NY 10580
(914) 967-0344

John T. Midyette III,
and Associates, Architects
1125 Canyon Road
Santa Fe, NM 87501
(505) 983-2639

Richard Mishaan Design
150 East 58th Street
New York, NY 10155
(212) 223-7502

John Oetgen Design Inc.
2300 Peachtree Road, NW,
Suite C-103
Atlanta, GA 30309
(404) 352-1112

Sarah Smith
152 East 79th Street
New York, NY 10021
(212) 327-4371

Stamps & Stamps
318 Fairview Avenue
South Pasadena, CA 91030
(626) 441-5600

Vermilion Designs Interiors
Bill Cook
1801 Friar Tuck Road, NE
Atlanta, GA 30309
(404) 874-4934

Bunny Williams, Inc.
306 E. 61st Street, 5th Floor
New York, NY 10021
(212) 207-4040

Linda Woodrum
T.S. Hudson Interiors
(843) 842-3663

The Adirondack Store
90 Main Street
New Canaan, CT 06840
(203) 972-0221

American Country Furniture
53 Old Santa Fe Trail
Santa Fe, NM 87501
(505) 982-1296

Artesanos Imports Co.
222 Galisteo Street
Santa Fe, NM 87501
(505) 983-1743

Austin International
815 Grundy Avenue
Holbrook, NY 11741
(800) 645-7303

Ballacchino Design
Custom Furniture
1333 McClendon Avenue
Atlanta, GA 30307
(404) 607-0455

The Bank Antiques
PO Box 275
Main Street
Searsport, ME 04974
(207) 548-6195

Bassett Furniture
3525 Fairystone Park Hwy.
Bassett, VA 24055
(866) 367-2608

Bed, Bath & Beyond
650 Liberty Avenue
Union, NJ 07083
(800) GO-BEYOND
www.bedbathandbeyond.com

Belcaro Fine Arts
Kathleen Scheinfeld
455 Lorraine Blvd.
Los Angeles, CA 90020
(323) 525-1805

Carriage Trade Antique Center
190 Main Street Center
Manchester, VT 05255
(802) 362-1125

Crate & Barrel
(800) 996-9960
(800) 323-5461 (catalogue)
www.crateandbarrel.com

Custom Metal Fabrication
K. Vincent Annaloro
2842 Franklin Street
Avondale Estates, GA 30002
(404) 296-4600

Donghia
979 Third Avenue
New York, NY 10022
(212) 935-3713

Door Store
One Park Avenue
New York, NY 10021
(212) 679-9700
www.doorstorefurniture.com

Editions
128 E. Marcy Street
Santa Fe, NM 87501
(505) 820-6148
editionsga@aol.com

Paul Ferrante, Inc.
8464 Melrose Place
Los Angeles, CA 90069
(323) 653-4142

Foreign Traders
202 Galisteo Street
Santa Fe, NM 87501
(866) 530-9080
www.foreigntraders.com

Galice Inc.
7916 Melrose Avenue
Los Angeles, CA 90046
(323) 655-7200

Gallery of Antique Costume
and Textiles
2 Church Street
Marylebone
London, NW8 8ED   England
(011) (44) 207-723-9981

Gilmartin Studio
1385 English Street
Atlanta, GA 30318
(404) 351-7886

Greenwich Tile & Marble Co., Inc.
388 West Putnam Avenue
Greenwich, CT 06831
(203) 869-1709

Homer
939 Madison Avenue
New York, NY 10021
(212) 744-7705
www.homerdesign.com

Indigo Seas
123 North Robertson Blvd.
Los Angeles, CA 90048
(310) 550-8758

Jackalope
2820 Cerrillos Road
Santa Fe, NM 87507
(505) 471-8539

Lloyd's Custom Furniture
8550 Melrose Avenue
Los Angeles, CA 90069
(310) 652-0725

Mario Villa Gallery
3908 Magazine Street
New Orleans, LA 70115
(504) 895-8731

McCormick Associates
PO Box D
Route 90
West Rockport, ME 04865
(207) 236-8528

Modernica
2118 E. 7th Place
Los Angeles, CA 90021
(212) 683-1963

Mohawk Industries, Inc.
PO Box 130
Sugar Valley, GA 30746
www.mohawkind.com

Monroe Salt Works Outlet Stores
Route 1
Belfast, ME 04915
(207) 338-3460

PierceMartin Atlanta
ADAC West, Suite B-2
349 Peachtree Hills Avenue
Atlanta, GA 30305
(404) 266-2619
www.piercemartin.com

Ralph Lauren Home Stores
650 Madison Avenue
New York, NY 10026
(212) 318-7000

Matthew Rao
SieMatic Corp.
351 Peachtree Hills Avenue, NE,
Suite 408
Atlanta, GA 30305
(401) 261-0008

Dyala Salam Antiques
174A Kensington Church Street
London, W8 4DP
England
(011) (44) 207-229-4045

Richard Schultz
Outdoor Furniture
806 Gravel Pike
PO Box 96
Palm, PA 18070-0096
(215) 679-2222

Gloria Slater Antiques
2115 Magazine Street
New Orleans, LA 71030
(504) 561-5738

Bill Steiner
Steiner Construction Co.
985 Camp Creek Drive
Lilburn, GA 30047
(770) 925-1482

Toad Hall
63 Pioneer Street
Cooperstown, NY 11326
(607) 547-4044

Wyndham Garden Hotel
6000 Pan American Freeway, NE
Albuquerque, NM 87109
(505) 821-9451

Y&B Bolour Carpets
321 South Robertson Blvd.
Los Angeles, CA 90048
(310) 274-6719

INDEX